THE LIFE OF JOHN BROWN

WITH SELECT WRITINGS

THE LIFE OF JOHN BROWN

WITH SELECT WRITINGS

Edited by

William Brown

THE BANNER OF TRUTH TRUST

THE BANNER OF TRUTH TRUST
3 Murrayfield Road, Edinburgh EH12 6EL
P.O. Box 621, Carlisle, PA 17013, USA

Previously published as *Memoir and Select Remains
of the Rev. John Brown*, Edinburgh, 1856
First Banner of Truth Edition, 2004

ISBN 0 85151 857 5

Printed and bound in Great Britain
by the Cromwell Press Ltd.,
Trowbridge, Wilts.

CONTENTS

FOREWORD

The *Life* (originally, *Memoir*) *of John Brown* now republished is the story of a Scottish shepherd boy who rose to become a revered minister and teacher of theology.

The son of poor parents, John Brown (1722–87) was orphaned at about the age of ten and supported himself at various times by working as as a shepherd, a pedlar and a school master. He taught himself Latin, Greek and Hebrew. He became the minister of the Haddington congregation of the Secession Church (Associate Synod), and later the Synod's professor, responsible for the instruction of all its ministerial students. His influence long lived on in his reference works, *The Self-Interpreting Bible* and the *Dictionary of the Bible*.

In 1964 the Trust republished the biography *John Brown of Haddington* by Robert Mackenzie, now out of print. This new book is not the same as the earlier work. The present book contains Brown's own account of his life, as edited and expanded by his youngest son, Dr William Brown, together with a selection of Brown's letters, his *Meditations* on important Christian themes, and his *Dying Advice to His Younger Children*.

Brown deserves attention as one of the brightest evangelical lights in Scotland in an age in which gospel truth was in danger of being eclipsed by Moderatism. Yet he himself was amazed to think that he had been used to do good to any: 'Oh! How strange that God should make use of one so sinful as I to do good to others!'

Towards the end of his pilgrimage, Brown exclaimed: 'Oh! What must Christ be in himself, when he sweetens heaven, sweetens Scriptures, sweetens ordinances, sweetens earth, and sweetens even trials! Oh! What must Christ be in himself!' May John Brown's *Life and Select Writings* help Christians today to live and die in the enjoyment of the same sweetness.

THE PUBLISHER
December 2003

PREFACE.

In preparing the following Memoir of my Father, it has been no way an object with me to raise a monument to his honour; my great design has been to produce a life which may be useful to the world. The applause of man—the breath of a worm that shall die—he never much cared for while living, and, I feel persuaded, that he now cares less for it than ever, unless it may be as a means of promoting the usefulness of his published works, by which " he being dead, yet speaketh."

A considerable portion of the volume has already passed through *five* editions, under the title of SELECT REMAINS, which were originally edited by my elder brothers, the Rev. John Brown of Whitburn, and the Rev. Ebenezer Brown of Inverkeithing, about two years after my father's death; and it is only proper that I should here state in what respects this differs from the former editions of the work, so as to warrant the change which I have made in the title. The short account which my father left of his life is here printed entire from a MS. which bears every mark of being a trustworthy copy of the original, on which, as formerly printed, some alterations had been made and some passages omitted, chiefly, I suppose, with the view of not giving offence in some quarters, but which I see no reason for now withholding. His "Dying Advice to his Congregation," and the "Narrative of his Dying Words," &c., which were originally separated from the Memoir, are now made to form part of it; but besides these, I have made considerable and not unimportant additions to it.

While the Memoir is thus greatly enlarged, and now forms the chief part of the volume, the other portions of the SELECT REMAINS are considerably diminished. I have omitted two or three of the Letters, and several of the Tracts or Meditations which originally formed part of the work, and a still larger portion of the matter introduced into the later editions. In doing this, I am satisfied I have not diminished, but increased the value of the work. It is not every thing that a good man has written which is worthy of being published; and articles of small value, even though printed, it is better to allow to pass into oblivion than to repeat them in every successive edition of a book. On the whole, I trust this will be found a useful work, not only to private Christians, but in a special manner to Ministers of the Gospel.

WILLIAM BROWN.

DUDDINGSTON, *April* 21, 1856.

MEMOIR

OF

THE REV. JOHN BROWN.

JOHN BROWN was born in 1722, at a place called Carpow, near Abernethy, a small town on the south side of the Firth of Tay. His father was of the same name, and was by trade a weaver; his mother's name was Catherine Millie. Not long before his death he drew up the following short memoir of his life :—

" The more I consider the dealings between God and my soul, I am the more amazed at his marvellous kindness to me, and my ingratitude and rebellion against him.

" It was a mercy that I was born in a family which took care of my Christian instruction, and in which I had the example of God's worship, both evening and morning ; which was the case of few families in that corner at that time. This was the more remarkable that my father, as I have heard, being born

B

under Prelacy, got no instruction in reading, or next to none, but what he got from masters after he began to be a herd.

"About the eighth year of my age, I happened in the crowd to get into the church on the sacrament Sabbath, when it was common for all but intended communicants to be excluded.* The table or tables which I heard served before I was shut out, were chiefly served upon Christ, and in a sweet and delightful manner. This captivated my young affections, and has made me since think that little ones should never be excluded from the church on such occasions. Though what they may hear may not convert them, it may be of use to begin the allurement of their hearts to the Saviour.

"My thirst after knowledge was great. My pride not a little instigated my diligence, particularly in learning by heart what catechisms I could get. I have found not a little advantage by this, especially by my learning of Vincent's and Flavel's Catechisms, and the Assembly's Larger Catechism. My parents' circumstances did not allow them to afford me any more but a very few quarters at school, for reading,

* This statement will appear strange to readers in Scotland of the present day, as in the Presbyterian churches, both Established and Dissenting, the general practice is for those who are not intending communicants to be present, when the Lord's supper is observed, equally as the communicants. How far the practice here referred to prevailed in former times, we do not know; neither can we say whether there are any districts of the country where it still prevails; but we never heard of any.

writing, and arithmetic; one month of which, without their allowance, I bestowed upon the Latin.

"My father dying about the eleventh year of my age, and my mother soon after, I was left a poor orphan, who had almost nothing to depend on but the providence of God.

"Meanwhile, in 1734, and especially in 1735, the Lord, by his Word read and preached, did not a little strive with and allure my soul. The reading of Alleine's 'Alarm to the Unconverted' contributed not a little to awaken my conscience and move my affections. Some of his hints, made worse by my mind, however, occasioned my legal covenanting with God. I made much the same use of Guthrie's 'Trial of a Saving Interest in Christ.' Indeed, such was the bias of my heart under these convictions, that I was willing to do any thing, but flee to Christ and his free grace alone for salvation. In these times I had no small delight in reading religious books, the Bible, Rutherford's Letters, and the like; and by means of these, particularly by means of Gouge's 'Directions how to walk with God,' was led into considerable circumspection in my practice. The sweet impressions made by sermons and books sometimes lasted several days on end, and were sometimes carried to a remarkable high degree. Under these I was much given to prayer, but concealed all my religious appearances to the uttermost of my power.*

* Of some of the circumstances here referred to, we have some further notices, in a letter dated August 6, 1745, when they must have been yet fresh in his memory : " After a

"Four fevers on end brought me so low within a few months after my mother's death, as made almost

formal slight using of Alleine's ' Directions for Conversion,' I dedicated myself to the Lord in solemn vow, as Alleine directs (summer 1735 or 1736); particularly, I vowed to pray six times in the day when I was herding, and three when I was not herding; so I continued to do this; and if I was deficient one day, I made amends the next. If I fell into any known sin, I prayed for forgiveness, and so was well. All movings of the affections I took for special enjoyings of God, and now thought myself sure of heaven, if I was not a hypocrite; to avoid which deceit, I kept the whole of my religion as hid as I could, especially prayer; and to that end prayed almost aye in the field, where, if I was not pretty sure nobody was near, I was exceeding low of voice; and lest my head being bare might discover it, I cast my blanket over it, or else laid an open book before me, that so they might think I was reading; and so made myself, in my conceit, as sure of heaven as possible. In this way of doing I continued from that time till June 1740, or else 1741 at least, if not till now; still putting my fashion of religion in Christ's room, setting up my formal prayers, &c., for my Saviour; yea, for my God." The distinction which he made as to the number of times he prayed when he was herding and when he was not herding, arose, no doubt, out of the circumstance that in the latter case it was scarcely possible for one in the station he was in, engaging in prayer without being observed by others,—in other words, that he had less opportunity for prayer in the one case than in the other.

We do not know it to be a fact, but we imagine that the two Meditations in the subsequent part of this volume, entitled, "Reflections of a Soul shut up to the Faith," and " Reflections of a Christian upon his Spiritual Elevations and Dejections," are substantially an account of his own religious experience.

every onlooker lose all hopes of my recovery; only I remember a sister, the most simple, but the most serious of all us children of the family, told me that when she was praying for me, that word, ' I will satisfy him with long life, and show him my salvation,' was impressed on her mind, which she said made her perfectly easy with respect to my recovery. Apprehensions of eternity, though I scarce looked for immediate death in these troubles, also affected me.

" But the death of parents, and my leaving a small religious family to go into a larger, in the station of a herd boy, for two or three years, was attended with not a little practical apostasy from all my former attainments. Even secret prayer was not always regularly performed, but I foolishly pleased myself by making up the number one day which had been deficient in another.

" It was my mercy, too, that in all my services I was cast into families, except perhaps one, where there were some appearances of the grace of God, beside useful neighbours.

" At length, after a multitude of ups and downs, glowings of affections, and sad coolings, I, after a sore fever in 1741, which somewhat awakened my concern about eternal salvation, was providentially determined, during the noontide, while the sheep which I herded rested themselves in the fold, to go and hear a sermon, at the distance of two miles, running both to and from it. The second or third sermon which I heard in this manner (and I had no other opportunity of hearing, the greater part of the

year) being preached on John vi. 64, 'There are
some of you that believe not,' by one I both before
and afterwards reckoned a most general preacher,
pierced my conscience as if almost every sentence
had been directed to none but me, and made me
conclude myself one of the greatest unbelievers in
the world. This sermon threw my soul into no
small agony and concern, and made me look on all
my former experiences as nothing but common operations of the Spirit; and in this manner I viewed
them for many years afterwards; and often in my
sermons, after I was a preacher, described the lengths
which common operations might go upon this footing.
But at last I began to doubt that I had been too
rash in throwing aside all my former experiences as
having nothing of the really gracious in them. And
I saw that it was improper for a preacher to make
his own experiences, either of one kind or another,
any thing like the discriminating standard of his
conceptions or declarations on these delicate subjects.

" On the morrow after, I heard a sermon on Isaiah
liii. 4, 'Surely he hath borne our griefs, and carried
our sorrows,' which enlightened and melted my soul
in a manner I had not formerly experienced; and I
was made as a poor lost sinner, the chief of sinners,
to essay appropriating the Lord Jesus as having done
all for me, and as wholly made over to me in the
gospel, as the free gift of God and my all-sufficient
Saviour,—answerable to all my folly, ignorance,
guilt, filthiness, wants, slavery, and misery. This

sermon had the most powerfully pleasant influence on my soul of any that I ever heard.

" By a sermon on Isaiah xlv. 24, ' Surely in the Lord have I righteousness and strength,' my soul was also remarkably affected and drawn to the Lord. By means of these and other ordinances, the sweetness which I had felt about 1735 was not only remarkably returned to me, but I had far clearer views of the freedom of God's grace, and of the exercise of taking hold of and pleading the gracious promises of the gospel.

" I had not lived much above a year after, amidst many delightful breathings of God's Spirit, intermingled with fears, temptations, and prevalencies of inward follies and corruptions together, when I was exercised with a new and sharp trial, especially on the account of the piety and influence of some that promoted it.

" By means of my anxious pursuit of learning, as I could get any opportunity, I had, by the Lord's assistance, acquired some knowledge of the Latin, Greek, and Hebrew languages, and was beginning to purpose to use it in the service of Christ, if he should open a regular door. My learning of these languages without a master, except for one month, occasioned some talk of me, and some small connection between some Seceding students and me, some of which proved my stedfast friends, while others took a very different course. Having no knowledge of polite manners, being never more than a bashful herd boy, I did not know the danger of saying the

truth. Accordingly, I was simply drawn into impart-
ing to an intimate friend a hint which was thought
not so honourable to one of the students, though I
meant nothing but a simple declaration of truth, in
answer to the question put to me by my friend.
This was represented by the student as false; my
words were misrepresented, as if they had borne that
I was as, if not more, learned than he; and to crown
my afflictions, it was represented by him and his
defenders that I had certainly got my learning from
Satan.

" As scarcely any person had ever appeared noted
for the knowledge of languages, but such as had
learned at least some of them by their own mere industry, it manifested either strong prejudice or great
ignorance of what had passed in the learned world,
to put this construction upon what my hard labour,
by the blessing of God, had acquired to me. It was,
however, thought necessary by the managers of it to
hunt me down with this malevolent reproach. Nor
did they spare to invent or hand about many mere
fictions of their own, in order to make it gain credit.*

* In the present day this will appear a very strange, not
to say ridiculous report; but in former times similar charges
were not unknown. " Roger Bacon, the greatest philosopher
of the thirteenth century, was reported to be addicted to
necromancy and the unholy ' communion of devils; ' and so
powerful were the secret intrigues of his enemies, that though
the heads of the University of Oxford, with which he was
connected, were friendly to his interest, it was deemed expedient, not only to prevent him from taking any share in the
instruction of the youth, but even to condemn him to a

" While for several years this calumny was carried on, and spread far and wide, I enjoyed remarkable mixtures of mercy with the affliction. In my very entry on it, that word, ' The Lord will command his loving-kindness in the day-time, and in the night his song shall be with me, and my prayer to the God of my life,' was peculiarly sweet to my soul. The members of the praying societies to which I belonged all continued my steady friends. Not one that I know of who knew me, as far as I discovered, appeared less, but rather more friendly to me than before, except such as were very nearly connected with the raisers or chief managers of the calumnious report. Nay, my acquaintance with the world being extended, many others upon my first acquaintance were remarkably sympathizing and friendly.

" Meanwhile, the Lord, by powerful and pleasant impressions of his Word on my heart, particularly at sacramental occasions at Dunfermline, Burntisland, Falkirk, and Glasgow, marvellously refreshed my soul, and made these years perhaps the most pleasant that ever I had, or will have on earth. Discourses on these texts,—Heb. x. 37 ; Ezek. xxxvii. 12 ; Psalm

rigorous confinement, aggravated by the harshest of privations, and uncheered by the offices of friendship."—*Edinburgh Encyclopædia*, Art. ROGER BACON. The second edition of the book, printed in 1462, of which copies were sold by Faust in Paris as manuscripts, was regarded by the Parisians as executed by magic.—*Ibid*, Art. PRINTING. As regards young Brown, the accusation was probably the compound result of ignorance, envy, and malignity.

xci. 2; and a Meditation on Psalm v. 7, were particularly ravishing.*

"Meanwhile, I was led out to ponder my own heart
and way, and made to see myself as bad before God
as a devil, and much worse. This I took God to be
calling me to by the reproach. These things made
me not a little content with my lot, and kept me
from labouring to expose my reproachers, or even to
defend myself, unless when I thought I had a plain
call. And I then and ever since have found that the
Lord most clearly delivered me and vindicated me,
when I made least carnal struggling, but laboured
to bear his indignation as quietly as I could. The
sting I had found in my learning which I had so
eagerly hunted after, tended to keep me humble
under what I had attained, or afterwards attained.
The reproach which I myself had met with, tended
to render me less credulous of what I heard charged
on others. On these and other accounts, I have since
looked on that sharp affliction as one of God's most
kind providences to my soul.

"During these trials I had my own share of solicitations to desert the Secession, in which I was so ill
used by some of the chief managers. But as I had
not taken that side from regard to men, the Lord
enabled me to take no offence at his cause, because
of their maltreatment of me.

"Micah vii. 7–10 had been not a little impressed
on my mind under my sore trial of about five years'

* "To some of these sweet transactions I allude in my
'Christian Journal of a Spring, Winter, and Sabbath Day.'"

continuance; and the Lord, by a connection of providences, gradually opened a way for my getting some regular instruction in philosophy and divinity, and I was licensed to preach the gospel in 1750; and I could not but be affected that about the same time, if not the very same night, my primary calumniator, and whose part had been so earnestly maintained in opposition to me, was, after he had been several years a preacher, and a zealous preacher in appearance, necessarily excommunicated by his supporters, as guilty of repeated acts, or attempts at acts, of uncleanness, even with married women. ' Behold,' O my soul, ' the goodness and severity of God, towards him severity, and towards me'—who was perhaps ten thousand times worse before His all-seeing eye— ' goodness.' Let me never be ' high-minded, but fear.'

" The morning before I was licensed, that awful scripture, Isaiah vi. 9, 10, ' Go, tell this people, Hear ye indeed, but understand not; and see ye indeed, but perceive not. Make the heart of this people fat, and make their ears heavy, and shut their eyes; lest they see with their eyes, and hear with their ears, and understand with their heart, and convert, and be healed,' was much impressed on my spirit; and it hath since been, I know not how often, heavy to my heart to think how much it was fulfilled in my ministry. I know not how often I have had an anxious desire to be removed by death from being a plague to my poor congregation. But I have oft taken myself, and considered this as my folly, and begged of

Him, that if it was not for his glory to remove me by death, he would make me successful in his work; for as to transportations I had not a good opinion of most of them, and I looked on it as so far my mercy that my congregation was so small.

" After all, I dare not but confess Christ to be the best Master I ever served. Often in preaching, and otherwise, I have found his words ' the joy and the rejoicing of my heart.' He hath often laid matter before me in my studies, and enabled me with pleasure to deliver it. God in our nature, and doing all for us, and being all to us,—free grace reigning through his imputed righteousness, — God's free grant of Christ and his salvation, and of himself in Christ,—and the believer's appropriation founded on that grant, and the comfort and holiness of heart and life flowing from that, have been my most delightful themes. And though I sometimes touched on the public evils of the day, yet my soul never so entered into these points.

"No sermons I ever preached were, I think, sweeter to my own soul than those on Psalm cxlii. 7, first clause; Isaiah xliv. 5, first clause; Isaiah xlvi. 4; Isaiah lx. 20, last clause; John xi. 28; 1 Timothy i. 15, 16; and Rev. iii. 21. The little knowledge which I had of my uncommonly wicked heart, and of the Lord's dealings with my own soul, helped me much in my sermons; and I observed that I was apt to deliver that which I had extracted thence, in a more feeling and earnest manner than other matters.

" And now, after near forty years' preaching of

Christ and his great and sweet salvation, I think that
if God were to renew my youth, and put it entirely in
my choice, whether I would be King of Great Britain,
or a preacher of the gospel, with ' the Holy Ghost
sent down from heaven,' who had to beg his bread
all the labouring days of the week, in order to have an
opportunity of preaching on Sabbath to an assembly
of sinful men, I would by his grace never hesitate
a moment to make my choice. By the Gospel do
' men live, and in it is the life of my soul.'

" When I consider what the Lord has done for me,
and what I have been doing against the Lord and his
goodness, I know not whether to be most amazed at
his kindness, or my rebellious treachery and ingratitude. God has been doing all that he can to save,
smile on, and favour me, and I have been acting to my
uttermost in opposing and dishonouring him. After
all that he has done for me, I am good for nothing,—
neither to teach nor learn, neither to live nor die ;—
but am both in heart and life evil—only evil—super-
abundantly evil, unto this very day. I am amazed
to think how the Lord hath concealed my weakness
and wickednesses, and even rendered them useful to
me. Considering the dreadful pride of my heart, what
a mercy that God who gave me learning in so unex-
pensive a manner, annexed for a time such a sting of
reproach to it ; that my talents did not lie so properly in a quick and extensive view of things at first,
(for in this I saw that I was inferior to many of my
brethren), but rather in a close, persevering, and un-
wearied application to what I engaged in ; that not-

withstanding all my eager hunting after most part of that lawful learning which is known among the sons of men, I was led generally to preach as if I had never read a book but the Bible. And the older I grew, I more and more aimed at this, (an observation which I had made in the days of my youth, that what touched my conscience or heart was not any airy flights or well-turned phrases, but either express scriptural expressions, or what came near to them), and led me to deal much in scriptural language, or what was near it. My imagination being somewhat rank and inclined to poetic imagery when I commenced a preacher, sometimes led me into flighty thoughts or expressions. But the Lord made me ashamed of this as a real robbing of him, in order to sacrifice to my own devilish and accursed pride. It was my mercy, too, that the Lord, who had given me some other talents, withheld from me a popular delivery, so that though my discourses were not disrelished by the serious as far as I heard, yet they were not so agreeable to many hearers as those of my brethren. It was a pleasure to me to observe many of my brethren possessed of that talent which the Lord, to restrain my pride, had denied to me.

"When I consider how many whose parents were spared with them far longer than I had mine, and whose station in the world and means of education were far greater than mine, are in deep poverty, or, which is infinitely worse, have been left to turn out abandoned rakes, I am amazed to think by what kind and strange means the Lord hath carried through the

poor young orphan till now, and taken him 'from
following the ewes with young,' and exalted him to
the highest station in the church of Christ, and by
his mere grace made somewhat useful, not only in
preaching and writing, but also in training up many
for the ministry, whom I hope the Lord hath, or will
make far more useful in winning souls to Christ than
ever I have been.   Notwithstanding he left me a
young orphan, without any relations on earth that
were able to help me to any purpose, he carried me
through to a larger stock of learning than many others
who had the greatest plenty; and all this without my
being obliged to be ever in debt to, or dependent on,
any person whatsoever.   In this how plainly hath
the Lord appeared as the 'Father of the fatherless,
and the orphan's stay.'   This kindness of the Lord
to me, as well as Psalm lxviii. 5, and cxlvi. 9; and
Jeremiah xlix. 11, encourageth me to leave my former
and present young family on him without the least
anxious care or fear.   I cannot leave them many
pence poorer than I was left myself; and though I
would wish that God would render them more holy
and useful in the world, I dare not wish them more
easy, or more honourable, or wealthy, than God hath
graciously made me.

" My vain curiosity hath led me into not a little
useless reading, to the mispending of much precious
time.   But even by this the Lord hath taught me
what a mercy it was, that when I had not a director in
the choice of books, nor money to purchase the best,
he hath led me into acquaintance with the most useful

ones, and did not permit me to take up with such as were erroneous or profane. From experience I have found, that it is vain to attempt to be a universal scholar; that a few books, well chosen, and carefully used, are better than a multitude of books; that multitudes of books are scarcely worth reading, or if read, one had better extract the useful hints into a note-book, and never more look into the books themselves; that abridging of more useful books, especially if they be large, is very useful; that few plays or romances are safely read, as they tickle the imagination, and are apt to infect with their defilement; and even those that are most pure, as of Young, Thomson, Addison, Richardson, bewitch the soul, and are apt to indispose for holy meditation, and other religious exercises, and so should be read, at most, but very sparingly. In reading histories, the Lord not only often made me take up the facts as the doing of the Lord, and as verifications of some part of his Word, but also made the stories to suggest some useful, and sometimes very sweet thoughts respecting the redemption scheme.

" Notwithstanding my minding earthly things, the Lord so managed my wicked heart that it has rather been my care to husband well what he provided for me, than to attempt a greedy catching of what did not come of its own accord; and notwithstanding my eager desire of books, I chose rather to want them, and much more other things, than run into debt. I have been helped to live as one that would gladly spend and be spent for my people, and aimed at seeking not theirs but them;—yet not I, but the grace of God did all. My congregation's belief of this, I believe, not only disposed them to regard me, but even readily to concur with me in countenancing the erection of other congregations within our original bounds, while some other congregations, perhaps double our strength, opposed as for life any such thing within their bounds. By this means I have now, in my old age, the pleasure of seeing the gospel fixed at Dunbar, North Berwick, and Tranent, all which places were in my original bounds, and I hope and heartily wish with more success than by me. This pleasure I would not lose for I know not how large an advancement of my stipend. And yet to the Lord's honour as well as that of my people, I have never lost a farthing by these disjunctions. I have always looked on it as a great and hurtful blemish in ministers, especially Seceders, to appear greedy of gain, as if they wanted to ' serve not the Lord Jesus, but their own belly ' and purse.

" I have also thought it a remarkable management of my mind by the Lord, that though I often grudged paying a penny or two for a useless letter, I could have cheerfully bestowed as many or more pounds for promoting a pious purpose. For this end I for many years laid aside a certain part of my income when I got it. I think this having of a distinct purse for the Lord is very proper. And from experience I can testify, that liberality to the Lord is one of the most effectual means of making one rich. I have sometimes disposed of more this way than it could be

C

thought I was capable of, and yet I never found myself poorer against the year's end. Nay, when I think on matters, I wonder that my wealth, instead of being diminished, is not a little increased. 'There is that scattereth, and yet increaseth; and there is that withholdeth more than is meet, but it tendeth to poverty.'

"I lament that I have been so deficient in effectual fervent prayer for my flock, and for the church of God; and that my discourse in conversation in my family, or with others, has not been more spiritual. My sense of my weakness and unskilfulness in pushing religious discourse, made me keep company so little; and when at any time I was in company without something serious, it was painful to me to reflect on it. It was on this account, as well as because I thought feasting improper on such occasions, that I much disrelished all feasting at the ordination of ministers, at baptisms, or on Mondays after the Lord's supper, as little else than an ordinance of the devil, calculated to erase every serious impression which had been made by the ordinance. I had little better opinion of making the disputes or curiosities of religion the subject of conversation, especially on the Lord's day.

" I lament that though I pretty often attended the Society meetings for prayer and spiritual conference, yet I did not do it more, especially after my settlement in the congregation. I am persuaded that ministers encouraging of such meetings to the most of their power, and their catechising and exhorting of children after their settlement, are some of the best means they can use for promoting the welfare of souls. On things of this nature, I would wish all ministers' zeal and care were chiefly spent.

" In public things, I have been rather inclined to act up to my own views than to push others into conformity with me. I had little relish for making ecclesiastical rules without great harmony. I had found no small difficulty in fixing my sentiments on some things. This made me averse to urge my opinions on others, unless where I had plain Scripture to support them. I laid it down as a rule, never to be very zealous in favour of any thing in which my own self-interest or honour was in any respect concerned. I found it was dangerous even in the lawful defence of self to go too far. My sense of the forwardness of my temper, and that several of my brethren saw more quickly or further into a cause than I did, restrained me from obstinacy in judgment. My knowledge of the miserable effects of clerical contentions in the Christian church, and my strong inclination to peace, I believe, sometimes led me to undue yielding or silence."

Such is the brief memoir which Mr Brown drew up of his life, not long before he died. Among other circumstances mentioned by him, is the singular fact that he acquired some knowledge of Latin, Greek, and Hebrew, without the help of a master, except for one month which he bestowed on the Latin. This is not unworthy of notice, as an example of

" the pursuit of knowledge under difficulties." But in the case of young Brown, the difficulties were much greater than will readily occur to the reader. Of Greek he learned something before he got a Greek grammar. Of the way in which he acquired the alphabet, he gives the following account in a Vindicatory letter which he wrote in reference to various points, particularly as to his having learned these languages from the devil:—

"I learned the letters from Orth. Tab. Gram., marginal words in Ovid, names in the New Testament; for reason told me that at least our unaccidented tongue could not much change names from what they were in the Greek: as, 1. Words authoritatively interpretated, as Eli lama sabachthani, Tabitha cumi, Siloam, Corban, Golgotha, Gabbatha, Emmanuel, Cephas, Aceldama; for, if these be changed in any language,—as for example, if Aceldama be made Acerdama, it would be false; for it would say,—1st. That the Jews called that place Acerdama. 2d. That Acerdama, *Hebraicé*, signifies a field of blood. And so in the matter of all words of this kind. 2. Words authoritatively called alien, as Abaddon, Armageddon. 3. Proper, obsolete, inequivalented names, as *Hebraicé*, Cainan, Arphaxad, &c., Luke iii., *Græcé*, Olympas, Priscilla, &c. 4. Names changed in one place from what they were in another, as Noah, Gen. x. 1,—Noe, Luke iii. Now, both being alike to our English, the reason of their change is the Greek; and, therefore, must be in the Greek as in ours. Now, all the Greek letters may be found by comparing Eloi lama sabachthani, Arphaxad,

        Ελωι λαμα σαϐαχθανι, Αρφαξαδ,

Capernaum, Sem, Aceldama, Booz, Ragau, and

Καπερναουμ, Σημ, Αϰελδαμα, Booζ, Ραγαυ,

Salmos.

Ψαλμος.

"Now, to prove the powers to be what you conceive or not, look other words : as for example, I would be sure of ϐ that it is equal to *b*,—I look Αϐρααμ, Αϐιουδ, Αϐια, Ωϐηδ, in all which, if I have hit right on the power ϐ by calling it *b*, then the second form in all these four words must be like it; but this is true; therefore the former. This way I used.

"Another rule I also walked by is, cast your eyes on what form you will, and fancy it to be what power you will; then compare it with other words having powers equivalent, and if they confirm it not, fancy it to be some other power, and so do till you find some words to confirm you in your fancy; and then you may take it for probable that you have really lighted on its power. And if it can be found to be no single letter, fancy it to be some double consonant, diphthong, or syllable; as for example, I cast mine eye on ϐ. I fancy it to be α. I look Aram, Asa, Josaphat, *Græcé*. I see nothing like it there; and yet the power α is there; *ergo*, it is not α. And, by the by, I remark that the power of α is found *Anglicé* four times besides capitals, and it only is so often found; but the Greek form α is found alone so oft; *ergo*, the form α has the power of *a* English. Again, I fancy ϐ to have the power of our *d* by comparing Αμιναδαϲ, Ωϲηδ, Αϲιουδ, Ελιουδ; I say the antepenult and ult letter in the other three is *d* English; therefore, the antepenult form in Aminadab and the other three *Grœcé* must have the power of *d*, by the rule anent obsolete names; but this form is δ, not ϲ; and so ϲ is not equal in power or sound to *d*. But observing such a form in Ωϲηδ,—now, the second power there is that of *b* English; therefore, I fancy it to be *b*, and by comparing it with Ζοροϲαϲελ, Ιακωϲ, I found it proven to be *b*.

"Thus one might go through all the forms. Now, I knew proper names from the places they are put in with us *Anglicé*, the initiating capitals, their repetitions, &c. As for the other ways I used, it would weary you to hear them; so I forbear at this time.

"When I had, by these means, got myself into a probability that I had the letters, I came down and sounded them before Mr Reid, and when he did not approve of my way, I called them his way, viz., n, u, &c.

"Now, the way I took to learn the sense was much the same, by comparing the Greek words with the words in our Testament, beginning at the shortest verses, as 1 Thess. v. 16, &c.; and as I had observed many terminations with some of their oblique cases in Latin Greek rudiments, so as I went along I made it my study to notice verbal terminations, right and oblique, still allotting them to that person, time, mood, voice, &c., their English agreed to. All this while, I never thought of its dual number, middle voice, &c., which the Latin has not. Also I noticed prepositions, adverbs, &c. As to construction, Ruddiman told me (Rud., p. 98, I think) that the Rules he has not distinguished by an asterisk are natural; therefore, I concluded, used in Greek. Some others I noticed, as Ακουω, 68, &c. All this time I got lessons now and then from Mr Reid; then I got a grammar and rudiments, &c. As for Hebrew, I got a grammar one hundred and ten days before I saw another Hebrew book, and am far from so exact in any of them as they (*i. e.*, his maligners) report." *

---

* As the above extract is from the letter already quoted, dated August 6, 1745, which was consequently written when he was about twenty-three years of age, the reader will readily excuse the faults of composition observable in it, when he considers that it was the production of a young man who had enjoyed very few advantages of education, and who, so far as he was self-educated, had devoted his attention chiefly to the dead languages, and, as is too common, was little practised in writing his own language.

It is related of him about this period of his life, that having gone to St Andrews, he went into a bookseller's shop and asked for a Greek Testament, and that a gentleman who was there at the time, (perhaps one of the professors in the University,) being struck with the circumstance of a young person of his appearance asking for such a book, made some inquiry at him as to what he wanted with it, and, on being told, said he would give it to him for nothing if he could read it, which he having done, obtained the invaluable gift. What truth there is in this anecdote we do not know ; but if there is any foundation for it, we imagine that the circumstances we have mentioned are all that can now be stated in regard to it. We

In April 1747, a division, commonly known by the name of the *Breach*, took place in the Secession Church in Scotland, to which young Brown had early attached himself. It had for some time past been

would scarcely, however, have noticed it at all, were it not for the following version which has been given of it:—

" Mr Brown, a respectable, though Seceding clergyman, in Haddington, not far from Edinburgh, being poor, when a boy, was employed in driving frequently the horses of a farmer in East Lothian. Having gone one day to Edinburgh, in company with many others, with grain to the market, while the horses were resting, and his companions sleeping beside them, Mr B. went to the Parliament Close, where he heard the cheapest books were to be found, in quest of a Greek Testament. The proprietor of the shop walking before the door when he passed, finding a poor ragged-like boy asking for a Greek Testament, inquired of him what he would do with it? 'Why, read it, if it please your honour.' 'Can you read it?' 'Why,' replied the boy, ' I will try.' Some of the shopmen having found one, put it into his hand, and the master said, 'If you can read it, you shall have it for nothing.' The boy took it, and having read a page, translated it with great ease. The bookseller would have no money, though the boy, who had pulled out half-a-crown from a purse in his pocket, urged him much to take it, knowing that to be the price of the book.

" About twenty years after this, a well-dressed man came up to the same bookseller, who, as formerly, was walking before his door, but with a wig and staff, saying—' Sir, I believe I am your debtor.' The bookseller said, ' I do not know; but step in and any of the young men will tell you.' ' But,' replied he, ' it is to you personally that I am indebted.' Looking in his face, he said, 'Sir, I do not know that you owe me any thing.' ' Yes, I certainly do. Do you recollect that about twenty years ago, a poor boy came and got a torn by violent internal dissensions, and now it was divided into two branches, the one commonly called Burghers, the other Antiburghers; the ground of the final quarrel being the lawfulness or unlawful-

Greek Testament from you, and did not pay for it?' 'Yes, perfectly,' replied the bookseller; 'I have often thought of it, and the boy was no sooner gone than I was angry with myself for not asking his name and where he resided.' 'I,' replied the clergyman, 'was the boy; my name is Brown, and I live at Haddington.' Upon which, looking again in his face, and giving him his hand, he said, 'Mr Brown, I am glad to see you; I have often heard of you. We have here in our shop, as they have in every University library in the kingdom, your Self-Interpreting Bible, your Church History, &c., &c., which have brought me as much money, and are more called for, than any books in my shop. Will you be so obliging as to dine with me?' This was done, and a lasting friendship contracted, while they discoursed of the days of former years."—*Bruce's Juvenile Anecdotes*, p. 196.

This story, bating the circumstances already mentioned, we have no hesitation in pronouncing a pure fiction. The reader can scarcely fail to observe the circumstantiality and even minuteness of the details, a circumstance which shows to what a length invention is sometimes carried. It is a melancholy example of the little regard to truth which is too common in what is called the Religious world. In order to give point to a story, or to make out an interesting narrative, to invest men, or bodies of men, with qualities which they never possessed, to serve personal interests, or to promote party ends, many persons have little or no conscience in drawing on their imagination, in indulging their invention, and in perverting or suppressing truth. It is truly painful to think that men professing Christianity can act so inconsistently with its precepts and its spirit.

ness of the Burgess oath in a few towns in Scotland.*
Revolutions in countries often affect not only the
condition of nations, but also that of individuals,—
ruining some and raising others to a place which
they could never otherwise have occupied. Dissensions and divisions in churches are, in the providence
of God, sometimes followed by similar results. Had
it not been for the breach in the Secession Church,
it may be questioned whether John Brown and his
descendants would not have been doomed to pass
their days in manual employments in the lower walks
of life, as it is not unlikely that the calumny as to
his having got his learning from the devil, and the
opposition which was raised against him on that and
other scarcely less creditable grounds, would have
proved an effectual bar to his getting forward to the
ministry. Among those who specially set themselves against him was the Rev. Alexander Mon-
crieff, one of the four ministers who originally con-
stituted the Secession from the Church of Scotland,
and who had now been for several years the professor of divinity to the Associate Synod,—a man not to
be easily thwarted in any purpose which he formed.
The Rev. Adam Gib, of Edinburgh, was also influenced against him, and so, probably, were likewise
others of the ministers who brought about the breach

* In 1820 these two parties were again united; and in
1847 a union was also effected between them and the Synod
of Relief, which took its rise in 1752. These three bodies,
thus formed into one, assumed the name of the United Presbyterian Church.

in the Secession Church, and who originally formed the Antiburgher body.

In consequence, probably, of the unpleasant circumstances in which he found himself at Abernethy, he left that place, and began to go about the country as a chapman or pedlar, it is likely in a very small way ; but according to the accounts given of him, this was a line of life for which he was little fitted. How long he followed it we do not know ; but it appears that in the year of the breach in the Secession Church (1747), and perhaps, as we have already hinted, in consequence of that event having cleared away the obstacles to his coming forward to the ministry, he engaged in teaching a school at Gairney Bridge, near Kinross, an employment which was at least more in unison with the strong bent of his mind towards learning. He afterwards removed to the Spittal, a village in the parish of Penicuik, where he was occupied in a similar way. He had also now an opportunity of prosecuting his studies in philosophy and divinity, in connection with the Associate Burgher Synod. Divinity he studied first under the Rev. Ebenezer Erskine of Stirling, and afterwards under the Rev. James Fisher of Glasgow, two of the original founders of the Secession Church.

In July 1751, Mr Brown having received a unanimous call from the Associate Congregation of Haddington, the county town of East Lothian, was ordained over it by the Presbytery of Edinburgh. As the practices of former times are not unworthy of being recorded, it may here be mentioned that on his settlement at Haddington, the following were the arrangements agreed on for his ministerial labours:— In the winter months, November, December, January, and February, there were two meetings on the Lord's day for public worship—one in the forenoon, when a lecture or exposition of Scripture, and a sermon were delivered, and another in the evening, when a sermon was preached. This was commonly called the Evening Exercise. In the other eight months of the year there were three meetings for public worship;—the first in the forenoon, commencing at ten o'clock, when a lecture and a sermon were delivered; the second in the afternoon, when a sermon was preached; and the third consisted of the Evening Exercise. Such numerous services must have been very oppressive to the minister, and very unprofitable to the hearers.

It was further agreed that the congregation should be visited once, and examined twice every year.* The Visitation of a congregation consisted in the minister, commonly accompanied by one of the elders, visiting on an appointed day, intimated on the previous Sabbath from the pulpit, the families of the members in a particular district, when he catechised, first, the heads of each household, and afterwards the children, relative to the doctrines and duties of religion; he then addressed an exhortation to them, and closed the visit with prayer. The Examinations were of a more public nature. On a day, often an evening, intimated in like manner from the pulpit, a diet of

* Minutes of Haddington Congregation.

examination, as it was called, was held for the members of the congregation residing in a particular
district, when they and their families were expected
to attend in the church, or in some other appointed
place, for the purpose of being examined in a similar
way. The Shorter Catechism of the Westminster
Assembly of Divines was commonly taken as a kind of
text-book for these examinations. The minister would
first of all call on one of the members to repeat a
question out of the catechism, and would then proceed to ask further questions explanatory and illus-
trative of it; and though the answers were often little
more than Yes or No, yet they afforded him an
excellent opportunity for communicating religious
knowledge to his people, and to others who might
choose to attend. These two exercises, the private
visitations and the public examinations of the families
composing congregations, were (provided they were
well conducted) admirably adapted to promote the
knowledge and influence of religion in our churches;
and we cannot but deeply regret that they have in
the course of the present century fallen so much into
disuse, especially the public examinations; and that
even the private visitations, where kept up, are often
only a shadow of what they were in former times.
Even then they might not be equally useful as the
course recommended by Baxter in his "Reformed
Pastor," and might not realise his views of dealing
with the people's consciences and hearts; but yet
they were well calculated to be useful to both ministers and people;—to the former by making them

acquainted with their hearers, and with the measure of their religious knowledge, and to the latter by communicating to them much useful instruction, and stirring them up to diligence in seeking after it.

The visitation of the sick was also a stated piece of ministerial duty. Mr Brown was diligent and conscientious in attending to this duty; not tedious, but according to his opportunities, frequent. When any of his hearers were in affliction, he visited them immediately on being informed of it; nor was he backward to show the same sympathy towards persons of any other denomination, on his understanding that a visit from him would be welcome.*

In 1756, Mr Brown introduced into his congregation the practice of observing the Lord's supper twice a-year.† Strange as it may seem, this was a daring innovation. Throughout the Church of Scotland the ordinary practice was to observe it only once a-year; and in this, as in many other things handed down from our forefathers, she was followed by the Secession Church. The services connected with the observation of the Lord's supper in Scotland were, and still are, a chief hindrance to its frequent observance in most of the Presbyterian churches, both Established and Dissenting. Will-worship is an evil against which they have entered many a solemn protest; yet it is not easy to point to a more remarkable example of will-worship than the manner in which they observe the Lord's supper, an ordinance which, as originally instituted by

* Posthumous Works of the Rev. John Brown, p. 31.
† Minutes of Haddington Congregation.

Christ, was characterised by the most beautiful and impressive simplicity. There was, first of all, a fast-day on the Wednesday or Thursday of the preceding week, which it was considered a duty to observe as strictly, and by some, perhaps, even more strictly than an ordinary Sabbath. On the Friday there was, at least in some places, what was called an Exercise. On the Saturday there were often three sermons, two in the afternoon without any intermission between them, and one in the evening. On the Sabbath, the Action sermon, as it was called (for what reason we do not know), was preached by the minister of the place. This he followed up by what were called the *debarrings*, an address usually consisting of the marks or characteristics of worthy and of unworthy communicants, as helps to them in self-examination, and of encouragement to the one to come forward to the Lord's supper, and of warning to the others to beware of partaking of it, lest they should " eat and drink judgment to themselves, not discerning the Lord's body." Having next read 1 Cor. xi. 23–32, as the divine warrant for the ordinance, he then offered up what was usually called the Consecration prayer, in the course of which he set apart so much of the bread and wine as might be used, from a common to a holy purpose. Meanwhile, a portion of the communicants took their seats in what were called the Table seats, which were situated in front of the pulpit, and usually ran the whole length of the church. The minister of the place now proceeded to address the communicants, commonly on topics connected

with the love of Christ, particularly as manifested in
his sufferings and death, with the view of exciting in
them sentiments and feelings suited to the ordinance.
He then put into the hands of the communicants at
the centre of the table, immediately before the pulpit,
first the bread, repeating the words of institution :
"Take, eat; this is my body, which is broken for you:
this do in remembrance of me;" and then the wine,
saying, "This cup is the new testament in my
blood : this do ye, as oft as ye drink it, in remembrance of me. For as often as ye eat this bread, and
drink this cup, ye do show the Lord's death till he
come." The bread and the cup then passed, under
the eye of the elders, from one communicant to
another, until the whole had partaken of them. The
minister now continued his address on the same or
similar topics as those already mentioned, or perhaps
on the duties specially arising out of them, or out of
the ordinance itself. Such is what is called in Scotland a Table service. Then followed a succession
of similar services, perhaps five or six in number,
or even, in some instances, so many as eight or ten,
by the ministers of other congregations, who, on such
occasions, were his assistants,—two, three, or four in
number, and in some instances, perhaps, six or seven.
Including the Psalms sung between the successive services, they might occupy about twenty minutes each.
After the table services were concluded, there was a
lengthened address by the minister of the place,
commonly in the way of application and improvement,
and the whole was closed with a sermon by one of

his brethren who were assisting, the whole occupying, without any interval, eight or nine hours, and in some cases a still longer period; while, during nearly all the time, the ministers, his assistants, were delivering one sermon after another from a wooden tent in the churchyard, or a neighbouring park. On the Monday forenoon the work was concluded with two sermons. This was designed to be a thanksgiving service. Besides all this, the minister of the place was considered as not in the way of his duty if he did not preach in his own pulpit on the Sabbath before and the Sabbath after the observation of the Lord's supper—the one as preparatory to, the other as an improvement of it.*

* There were cases in which the number and extent of the services in connection with the Lord's supper was much greater than we have stated. In the congregation of the Rev. James Fisher at Glasgow, one of the four founders of the Secession, "there were at the administration of the Lord's supper usually *seventeen* or *eighteen* table services," "and the communion service, which commenced at *nine* or *ten* in the morning, did not close sometimes till between *nine* and *ten* in the evening."

The following abstract of the services in Mr Fisher's congregation, Glasgow, in connection with the observation of the Lord's supper, in June 1761, is taken from one of his note-books:—

Thursday: (Fast-day) forenoon, two sermons; afternoon, one sermon.

Friday: Evening, one sermon.

Saturday: Within, (the church) two sermons; without, (tent) two sermons; evening exercise.

It may here be proper to add that the congregations which collected on these sacramental occasions, as they were called, were not confined to the minister's ordinary members and hearers. It was customary for numbers of people,—in some cases, where the ministers were particularly popular, for multitudes,— to collect from various places, sometimes even from great distances. Many, especially during the summer, would attend upon them in various places, and would in this way communicate perhaps eight or ten times, though probably they would have risen up in arms

Sabbath : Besides the action sermon and its appendages, there were *eighteen* table services. The whole began at half-past nine in the morning, and ended at half-past nine in the evening, thus occupying twelve hours.

Besides these services within the church, there were *nine* sermons preached by *seven* different ministers at the tent.

Monday : Within, two sermons; without, two sermons.

It would thus appear, that including the action sermon and the evening sermon on the Sabbath, there were no fewer than *twenty-four* sermons preached on this " sacramental occasion," to which have to be added the table and other services connected with it.

On another occasion (1756) there were *seventeen* table services, and 1286 communicants.—*Memorials of the Rev. James Fisher, by John Brown, D.D.* Edinburgh: 1849.

There were some other places to which the flockings were very great, and at which the number of services and of assistant ministers must have corresponded; for example, Stirling in the days of Ebenezer Erskine, and Dunfermline in the days of his brother, Ralph Erskine.

against any proposal for the more frequent observation of the Lord's supper in the congregations with
which they were immediately connected. This practice of attending on sacramental occasions was much
cherished and increased by the circumstance that the
congregations of the ministers assisting at them were
often left without sermon, thus sacrificing the ordinary interests of several congregations for the sake of
the observance of the Lord's supper in some single
congregation. We may add, that to attend on sacramental occasions in other congregations than their
own, was one of the religious fashions of the day;
and it may be doubted whether one would have been
considered as truly pious who did not follow, in this
respect, the fashion of the day.

Such was, in former times, and such still is, in
its main outlines, the Scottish communion service in
the great body of the Presbyterian churches in this
country. Let any one compare it with the original
institution of the Lord's supper as recorded in the
New Testament, and then say whether there is so
much as a shadow of authority for it in the Word of
God. In truth, it is nothing more than a vain attempt of man to mend the work of God; and that
in reference to the most solemn and interesting
ordinance appointed by the Redeemer—the com-
memoration of his dying love; but here, as in other
cases, it will be found that " the foolishness of God
was wiser than man, and the weakness of God stronger
than man."

One of the results of the multiplied services con-

nected with the observation of the Lord's supper in
the Presbyterian churches in Scotland, was the in-
frequency of its observance. After all, however, it
may be made a question whether the increased frequency of the Lord's supper in many churches, is at
all desirable, or would be any improvement. If the
great body of the members of a church are unconverted persons, the seldomer they observe the Lord's
supper, it will for their own sakes be so much the
better, seeing they would thereby only "eat and
drink judgment to themselves, not discerning the
Lord's body." There are many churches as to which
it may fairly be made a question, whether the
Redeemer is more honoured or dishonoured by the
observation of this ordinance. Such churches, in
fact, are not rare in what is called the Christian
world. Purity of communion is one of the great
desiderata in most churches, both in our own and in
other countries.*

* Various modifications of the manner of observing the
Lord's supper in Scotland, as above described, have been
made in later times. In few places, if in any, is the Friday
Exercise now kept up. The number of sermons on the Saturday and Monday is, at least in many places, reduced to a
single sermon on each day; and the services of the Sabbath,
though retaining the same form as before, are less protracted
than they were. There is no longer that travelling to sacra-
ments in other places which once so much prevailed; the
tent sermons on the Sabbath are generally given up; and, as
a consequence of all this, fewer ministers are required as
assistants at them.

In the latter part of the last century, the practice of a some-

In 1758, Mr Brown made his first appearance as an author. The work which he published was entitled, " An Help for the Ignorant: Being an Essay towards an Easy Explication of the Westminster Confession of Faith and Catechisms, composed for the Young Ones of his own Congregation." On the publication of this volume (for a volume it was, of nearly 400 pages), a great outcry was raised against it by some

what more frequent observance of the Lord's supper was introduced into a few chapels connected with the Church of Scotland; for example, Lady Glenorchy's Chapel, Edinburgh, where it was observed six times a-year. In these *extra* cases, the whole of the week-day services were laid aside, with the exception of one evening sermon.

The practice of observing the Lord's supper twice a-year, introduced by Mr Brown into his own congregation, afterwards became general in that branch of the Secession Church with which he was connected. About the beginning of the present century, some of the congregations in our larger towns began to observe it four times a-year, laying aside, in a great degree, the accustomed week-day services on the two *extra* occasions; and their example was gradually followed by a number of congregations in the country. There are now some congregations in which it is observed six times a-year, and in which the whole of the communicants sit down at once to the sacred feast, as is customary in the Independent churches, which assuredly is the natural and scriptural mode of observing the ordinance.

I am at once pleased and surprised to see the sentiments entertained by my father as to the days connected with the observation of the Lord's supper in this country. They show how early and how much he had risen above the prejudices of the age in which he lived. In a small piece, written probably about this time, but not published till near twenty

few of the Antiburgher brethren, as containing new
and strange doctrine; even the heavy charges of
heresy, blasphemy, and the like, were not spared.
A pamphlet by the Rev. Mr Dalziel of Earlston,
was characterised by peculiar bitterness and asperity.
In his Catechism, Mr Brown had taught that though
Christ's righteousness is infinitely valuable in itself,
yet it is imputed to believers only in proportion to

years after his death, he thus expresses himself:—" I am not
averse to the custom of a fast preparation, and a thanksgiving day, *if the exercises on these days are considered as
means for encouraging strangers to attend,* AS THEY HAVE IT SO
SELDOM AT HOME; and when they are considered *as means* for
deepening *the solemnity of the approach to God in this ordinance,*
which in *our present case is quite,* or next to quite worn off,
in the long intervals between ordinances of this nature. But
is it not plain, that in case the church were returned to the
primitive custom, *there would be no need to encourage strangers
to attend,* because they would have *weekly* opportunities for
partaking at home? *And there would be less need to use means
of this nature to fix or deepen these impressions;* the conscientious
approach to God in this solemn ordinance, the Sabbath before
and the Sabbath after, would more effectually prepare the
soul for receiving and rivetting divine impressions than all
the work of these three days.

" When these days' exercises are considered as well-meant
human helps, *during the present unfrequency of administration,*
nobody regards them more than I do; but if anybody considers them, *as too many ignorant people do,* as essential parts
of this ordinance, and plead the *absolute necessity* of them, as
a reason against the more frequent administration of the supper,
can I, in consistency with our Confession of Faith, chap.
xxi. sect. 1, refrain from *detesting* that view of them, and the
usage proceeding therefrom, as *refined* POPERY? Are they not

their need, and to the demands which the law has upon them, so as to constitute them as perfectly righteous in law as the law requires them to be, but not in such proportion as to render them infinitely righteous. His assailants, on the other hand, maintained, that in justification the righteousness of Christ is imputed to us in its *whole infinite value,* as it is formally the righteousness of a God-man, so as to

of *human* invention? Was not the invention of them merely occasional? Are they not still unknown in many Protestant churches? Were they not unknown in the Church of Scotland for about seventy years after the Reformation? Do we not find one of our best Assemblies, namely, that of 1645, prohibiting to have any more than one sermon upon Saturday and another upon Monday? Did not Mr Livingston, as long as he lived, refuse to allow any more sermons on the Saturday and Monday at his sacramental occasions? Now, is it not plainly *Popish* to count *human* inventions and occasional additions, *essential* parts of this great ordinance?

" Besides, is it reasonable to plead the *necessity* of these exercises to the *extrusion* of a divine ordinance? What would we think of the man who, when he had opportunity to hear sermons on Sabbath but twice in the year, had thought meet to appoint a fast-day in his family, a preparation-day on Saturday, and the Monday for thanksgiving, on each of these occasions, if afterwards, when he might have sermon every Sabbath, he should refuse it, giving this as the reason, that he could not every week get three days set apart to the Lord, and that without this it would be a profanation to wait upon public worship, and the want of these would deprive him of all due impressions of this ordinance? The case is exactly parallel. Family worship approaches as near the solemnity of public hearing the word and public prayers, as hearing of sermons doth to that of communicating. Setting apart these constitute us, in law-reckoning, as *infinitely righteous* as the person of Christ God-man.*

We acknowledge we have no liking to such statements, either on the one side or the other; the Scriptures enter into no explanations or distinctions of this kind, and we feel it to be of paramount importance to keep close to the simplicity of holy writ. The speculations, reasonings, and conclusions of men

three days for family worship on such occasions, is merely a *human* contrivance; and so also is the setting apart these days on sacramental occasions. Setting apart these three days for family devotion, in the above circumstances, might be very expedient, and may have the signal countenance of God. But could this man's three days of family devotion be lawful,—could it be blessed of God, if adhered to as a reason for neglecting to attend on public worship through the other Sabbaths of the year?

" In fine, whether is it grace or corruption that most affects to add human devices to God's worship, in order to make it more splendid than Christ has left it? May not persons be as really *guilty of* POPERY by doting on the *splendid* pomp of divine ordinances that consists in the variety of days, sermons, and ministers, as by doting on the variety of fantastic ceremonies used in *the Popish Mass?* Ought we not to beware of adding to God's ordinances, as well as of taking from them? Is God content to barter with us in this point, by giving up with the frequent administration of the Supper, if we will annex a few more days' sermons, ministers, and people to it, when seldom administered? Where does he either make or declare his acceptance of this proposal?"—*Apology for the more frequent Administration of the Lord's Supper.*

* Brief Dissertation concerning the Righteousness of Christ. By John Brown. 2d Edit., pp. 3–6.

may gain for them the character of learned and deep
divines; but for our part we prefer a few plain
passages of Scripture to all their lucubrations, however ingenious and plausible they may be. The
questions which they raise have often a reference to
truths, the nature and relations of which are very
imperfectly understood by man, and in regard to
which it is very unsafe for a creature of such narrow
capacity and such limited views, to indulge in his
vain and shortsighted reasonings. If in past ages
the ministers of Christ had adhered closely to the
simplicity of Scripture, the world would have been
saved the agitation of numberless questions which
have gendered strifes, and divisions, and hostility
among those who might otherwise have been united
in the faith and love of the truth. In the present
instance we may remark, that while we apprehend
the New Testament enters into no such statements
as those made by Mr Brown, they yet appear natural
and reasonable from what we do find in Scripture;
while those of his assailants are not only without any
scriptural authority, but are unnatural and illogical
conclusions from the statements which we do find in
holy writ.

We would scarcely, however, have thought it worth
while to notice the matter at all, had it not been that
it gave occasion to an exemplification of the Christian
temper of Mr Brown which is not undeserving of
mention. In vindication of his sentiments he published a small pamphlet, entitled, " A Brief Dissertation concerning the Righteousness of Christ;" and

in the preface to it, after stating his own views on the points in question, he adds: " I have much more charity for the ministers of that party than to suspect the bulk of them are capable of imbibing, even through inadvertency, an old Antinomian and Familistic error; or have so small acquaintance with the writings of Protestant divines, as to imagine that I am the first who ever asserted that Christ's infinite righteousness is imputed to believers *precisely in proportion to their need,* and the demands of the broken law on them, or so as to make them perfectly and completely righteous in law, but not *in such proportion* as to render them *infinitely* holy, righteous, comely, or valuable in law; and had these few, who, it seems, are otherwise disposed, signified their scruples to me in a Christian manner, either by word or writ, I doubt not but I should have offered them such replies and solutions, as might have prevented that conduct, which (though charity obliges me to hope, was entirely an inadvertent and well-designed mistake,) some will readily reckon a wounding of truth, a dishonouring of Christ, an instructing of their people to revile, and in the issue, an injuring of their own reputation among impartial men. But now that the fact is committed, though I reckon it my duty to contribute my weak endeavours towards the support of injured truth, and to restore to the Scriptures and the most eminent Protestant divines, their due honour of being my instructors in this point, yet, instead of intending to resent, with similar conduct, the injury these reverend brethren have

done me, I reckon myself, on account thereof, so much
the more effectually obliged by the Christian law to
contribute my utmost endeavours towards the advancement of their welfare, spiritual or temporal,—
and am resolved through grace to discharge these
obligations, as Providence shall give opportunity for
the same. Let them do to or wish me what they
will, may their portion be redemption through the
blood of Jesus, even ' the forgiveness of sins, according to the riches of his grace; ' and call me what
they please, may the Lord call them ' the holy ones,
the redeemed of the Lord, sought out, and not forsaken ' ! " *

We may here also take occasion to notice other
instances of his forgiving spirit. Notwithstanding
the ill-usage which he had received from certain
ministers in the early stage of his studies, it was
remarked that he was never heard to speak evil of
them, nor so much as to mention the affair. The
Rev. Mr A., the Antiburgher minister in Haddington, who had treated him rudely, being reduced to
poverty, he sent him money, though in a way which
concealed the donor; and on his decease he offered
to take one of his destitute orphans, and bring him
up with his own children.†

" There is something very bewitching in authorship," says Caraccioli, " and he who has once written
will write again." Mr Brown having commenced

* Dissertation concerning the Righteousness of Christ,
p. 3.

† Posthumous Works, p. 35.

author, proved no exception to this remark. In the course of his subsequent life he published a great number of works, and on a variety of subjects. He was perhaps the most voluminous religious writer of the day in Scotland. Some of his writings, during his lifetime, and still more since his death, passed through numerous editions, particularly his " Self-interpreting Bible," his " Dictionary of the Bible," his " Concordance to the Holy Scriptures," his " Christian Journal," his Catechisms, both his large Explication of the Shorter Catechism already mentioned, and his two small Catechisms. Some of them have had extensive circulation not only in Scotland, but also in England, and in the United States of America.*

* The following is a list of Mr Brown's writings, arranged according to their subjects :—

Of the Holy Scriptures.

The Self-interpreting Bible, 2 vols. quarto, 1778.

A Dictionary of the Bible, 2 vols. 8vo, 1769.

A Brief Concordance to the Holy Scriptures, 1783.

The Psalms of David in Metre (Scotch Version), with Notes exhibiting the connection, explaining the sense, and for directing and animating the devotion, 1775.

Of Scripture Subjects.

Sacred Tropology; or, A Brief View of the Figures and Explication of the Metaphors contained in Scripture, 12mo, 1768.

An Evangelical and Practical View of the Types and Figures of the Old Testament Dispensation, 12mo, 1781.

" Them that honour me," said God to Eli, " I will honour ; but they that despise me shall be lightly esteemed." Seldom has the first part of this declaration been more signally fulfilled than in the case of Mr Brown. His great object in writing and publishing books was not the vanity or pride of authorship ; neither was it the desire of honour from his

The Harmony of Scripture Prophecies, and History of their Fulfilment, 12mo, 1784.

Systematic Divinity.

A Compendious View of Natural and Revealed Religion, 8vo, 1782.

Church History.

A General History of the Christian Church, from the Birth of our Saviour to the Present Time, 2 vols. 12mo, 1771.

A Compendious History of the British Churches in Scotland, England, Ireland, and America, 2 vols. 12mo, 1784.

An Historical Account of the Rise and Progress of the Secession, 12mo, 1766.

Biography.

The Christian, the Student, and Pastor, exemplified in the Lives of Nine Eminent Ministers in Scotland, England, and America, 12mo, 1781.

Practical Piety exemplified in the Lives of Thirteen Eminent Christians, and illustrated in Cases of Conscience, 12mo, 1783.

The Young Christian ; or, The Pleasantness of Early Piety, 12mo, 1782.

Catechisms.

An Essay towards an easy, plain, practical, and extensive Explication of the Assembly's Shorter Catechism, 12mo, 1758.

fellow-men, nor yet of making of money. His great design was to promote the glory of God and the good of souls. Few men, perhaps, have, in this respect, been more single in their aims : unless with a view to usefulness, we question whether he would ever have printed a single book. But though he sought not the honour that cometh from men, he received it in an eminent degree. It was not confined to his own denomina-

Two Short Catechisms, mutually connected, 12mo, 1764.

The Christian Journal; or, Common Incidents Spiritual Instructors, 12mo, 1765.

Sermons.

Religious Stedfastness recommended, 12mo, 1769.

The Fearful Shame and Contempt of those Professed Christians who neglect to raise up Spiritual Children to Christ, 12mo, 1780.

The Necessity and Advantage of Earnest Prayer for the Lord's special direction in the choice of Pastors, 12mo, 1783.

Miscellaneous Pamphlets.

A Brief Dissertation concerning the Righteousness of Christ, 1759.

Letters on the Constitution, Government, and Discipline of the Christian Church, 12mo, 1767.

The Re-exhibition of the Testimony Vindicated in opposition to the unfair account given of it by the Rev. Adam Gib, 8vo, 1780.

The Oracles of Christ and the Abominations of Antichrist Compared; or, A Brief View of the Errors, Impieties, and Inhumanities of Popery, 12mo, 1779.

The Absurdity and Perfidy of all Authoritative Toleration of Gross Heresy, Blasphemy, Idolatry, and Popery in Britain, in Two Letters to a Friend, 12mo, 1780.

tion, nor yet to his own country, nor to his own lifetime. The name of JOHN BROWN of HADDINGTON has become one of the honoured names in the Church of Christ. So far as earthly honour is of any value, he has received a rich and abundant reward.

Even Burns has *honoured* him with a niche in one of his poems, associating him with other two men in whose company one might well glory to be found:—

> " For now I'm grown so cursed douce,
>   I pray and ponder butt the house ;
>   My shins, my lane, I there sit roastin',
>   Perusing Bunyan, Brown, and Boston."

Thoughts on the Travelling of the Mail on the Lord's Day, 12mo, 1785.

Since his death the following have been published :—

Select Remains, 12mo, 1789.

Posthumous Works, 12mo, 1797.

Apology for the more frequent Administration of the Lord's Supper, 1804.

It will be seen from this list that there was much of system in his writings. They consisted, in fact, of *classes* of works of various kinds. Besides the two works on Church History which he published, he at one time contemplated a third, to contain a history of the Protestant churches of Switzerland, France, Holland, Germany, Denmark, Sweden, Poland, and Hungary, which would have nearly completed a system of ecclesiastical history. It is also worthy of notice how little his writings were of a controversial nature. Though he wrote so much, and lived in an age when controversy was rife, yet he seldom mingled in the strife. The great object which he ever had in view was the improvement of his readers in religious knowledge, and especially in personal piety.

As to making money by his writings, he appears never to have thought of it. He gave them to the publishers for nothing, hoping thereby to have them sold at a cheaper rate for the sake of the poor. Publishers and booksellers must have divided among themselves many thousand pounds, as profits derived from his writings, while he himself, strictly speaking, never derived a farthing from them; and his family, after his death, received only a very inconsiderable sum.*

The learning of Mr Brown was very considerable. His knowledge of languages will appear the more extraordinary, when it is considered that he never enjoyed the assistance of a teacher, except for about a month at the Latin. He was, notwithstanding, a

---

* One of his publishers, of his own good will, presented him with £25 or £30.* This sum he lent to the publisher of the first edition of his Bible, it being an expensive work to print. He, however, lost it; the publisher, we understand, having failed. After his death, his widow received £90 for several of his works corrected by himself, and some MSS.

Though, in regard to his writings, it must be admitted he acted disinterestedly, it cannot be said that he acted wisely. He himself and his family would have been much the better of receiving a fair portion of the fruits of his labour. Nor can it be alleged that, in receiving this, he would have been less " serving the Lord Christ." He might, on the contrary, have served him more effectually, and been useful in ways in which he was not otherwise able to be. The argument of the apostle (1 Cor. ix. 3–14) is as applicable to the *writings* as to the ordinary labours of ministers.

* The sum has also been stated as £40.

good Latin scholar. Of Greek, but especially of Hebrew, he possessed a critical knowledge. He could read and translate the French, Italian, Dutch, and German languages; and also the Arabic, Persic, Syriac, and Ethiopic. He gave attention to natural and moral philosophy, but his favourite reading was history and divinity, his knowledge of which is sufficiently testified by his writings. His acquaintance with the Bible was singular. Seldom was a text referred to but he could repeat it, explain its meaning, and point out its connection with the context.* But, though somewhat of a universal scholar, he made no display of his learning. It would almost seem as if he studiously concealed it. It is, we think, a defect in some of his writings, particularly those which relate to matters of fact, that he so seldom refers to his authorities. This probably arose, in a great degree, from a wish to avoid every thing like exhibition or display.

The example of Mr Brown furnishes singular encouragement to students of divinity, and to ministers of the gospel. His intellectual attainments were not the result of any great original genius. He was, no doubt, endowed with respectable talents; but he did not possess what is commonly called genius. He was no way distinguished by the faculty of imagination or invention, nor yet with any special powers of reasoning. It is to be regretted, we think, that he did not cultivate these higher faculties more. The leading powers of his mind were memory and judg-

* Posthumous Works, p. 26.

E

ment, exercised in patient, persevering, laborious, prayerful study. This was the secret of whatever attainments he made; and any one who will pursue a similar course need not despair of making similar attainments. He was, in fact, a striking example of the truth of that observation of Sir Thomas F. Buxton: "I hold as a doctrine, to which I owe not much, indeed, but all the little success I ever had,—viz., that with ordinary talent and extraordinary perseverance, all things are attainable." He had also fancy, but it was not always guided by judgment and good taste, and sometimes was allowed to run wild. On no subject did he give the reins so much to his fancy, as on what he considered the types of the Old Testament. Had he been more conversant with our best English writers, his own intellectual character might have been much improved, and his writings been more extensively and more permanently useful.

In 1768, Mr Brown was chosen by the Associate Burgher Synod their Professor of Divinity, upon the death of the Rev. John Swanston of Kinross. This was an office for which he was, in many respects, singularly qualified. He possessed not only the theological knowledge and learning, but the earnest piety and the deep sense of the solemn responsibility of the ministerial office, which are of such special importance in one who is employed in training up others "to feed the church of God, which he hath purchased with his own blood." *

In fulfilling the duties of this important office, he was little, if at all, in the habit of delivering lectures

* Acts xx. 28.

to his students. His instructions he communicated chiefly in the way of examinations. Several of the works which he published were prepared with a special view to the improvement of his students, particularly his " Compendious View of Natural and Revealed Religion," his " General History of the Christian Church," his " History of the British Churches," and his " Christian, Student, and Pastor." Previous to the printing of the first of these works, each student was, in the course of his attendance at the Divinity Hall, required to write out a copy of it. The manual labour of this could scarcely fail to be irksome, yet it would at least be attended with the advantage of deepening the impression of its contents on their minds. On this work they were subjected to careful examination ; and they were required to commit to memory, and to repeat the numerous passages of Scripture which are referred to in it, in support of the various positions laid down in it.*

* We have never been able to see the use of every Professor of Divinity giving a course of lectures on theology to his students ; and the remark may be extended to other branches of knowledge. Where experiments or demonstrations have to be exhibited to the eye, as in natural philosophy, chemistry, anatomy, botany, &c., lectures must, of course, accompany them ; but where no experiments or demonstrations are necessary, unless a professor has something new and important to communicate, or unless he has a clearer, more powerful, and more effective way of teaching than his predecessors, the reading by the students of the best standard works on the subject, or on the main topics of the course, and subjecting them to a strict examination upon them, will be found a much more effective method of teaching, as regards the mere communication of knowledge, than the reading

While he laboured to communicate to his students a systematic knowledge of divine truth, he was no less anxious to impress their consciences and hearts with a sense of their own individual interest in it, with the necessity of personal piety, and with the solemn responsibilities of the Christian ministry for which they were preparing. Of this, the address to his students in the beginning of his "View of Natural and Revealed Religion," and the appeals to them at the end of the several chapters of that work, are a striking example. At the close of the annual sessions of the Hall, he was also in the practice of addressing them on the subject of personal religion; of lectures to them,—the professor, in the course of his examinations, supplementing what he may think wanting in the books thus read, and pointing out any statements or reasonings which he may judge incorrect or fallacious. It will add greatly to the efficacy of this plan of instruction, if the students, after they have read and been examined on a particular subject, are required to draw out a synopsis of the whole matter or argument, whether contained in one or more works. We are well aware that the acquisition of knowledge, though very important in its own place, is not the only, nor perhaps the chief object to which education should be directed. This should, in a special manner, be the cultivation of the student's own faculties. We would do nothing to repress genius or original talent; on the contrary, we would do every thing to foster and cherish them. We would do nothing to check a student in the search after truth ; on the contrary, we would do every thing to encourage him in free, honest, independent inquiry,—" to dig for it as for silver, and to search for it as for hid treasures," —accompanying his inquiries with earnest and humble prayer to God to " lead him into all truth."

and his appeals on these occasions were often characterised by singular earnestness and solemnity.
Of these parting addresses, the following is an
example :—

"Thinking this morning on your departure, two
passages of Scripture came to my mind, and you
would do well to take them into your serious consideration: 'Have not I chosen you twelve, and one
of you is a devil?' One may be called to special
service,—may fill a public station in the church,—
may be a preacher,—may go abroad into the world,
and address people on things of deep and everlasting importance, and yet be a devil,—may be
under the power of Satan,—in a state of enmity
against God,—may be a traitor at heart, and act the
part of an open traitor at last,—may betray the
Master he professed to serve, and come to shame and
disgrace. Jesus knoweth all things; he 'searcheth the heart, and trieth the reins of the children of
men.' What state you are in,—what are the reigning principles in your breasts,—what are the motives
by which you are influenced, and what the ends you
have in view,—whether you are, indeed, what you
profess, and what your outward appearance would
indicate,—all is known to him. To commend a
Saviour for whom one has no love,—to preach a
gospel which one does not believe,—to point out the
way to heaven, and never to have taken one step in
that way,—to enforce a saving acquaintance with
religion, and to be an entire stranger to it one's self,
—how sad, how preposterous! Tremble, O my soul,

at the thought,—still more at the thing! Better
follow the meanest occupation than enter into the
holy ministry solely or chiefly for some secular or
selfish design. While I would be far from setting
limits to the divine sovereignty, I am afraid it but
seldom happens that a person is converted after he
becomes a preacher. Was there a Judas, a devil
among the twelve? What if there shall be one for
every twelve among you? 'Lord, Is it I?—Is it
I?—Is it I?'

" The other passage comes more closely home, and
is still more alarming: ' And five of them were wise,
and five were foolish.' Is it only one-half of the
number here present who are wise,—who are truly
serious, prudent, and thoughtful,—wise unto salvation; who are savingly instructed in the mysteries
of the kingdom, in whom Christ is found, and in
whose hearts he dwells by faith; who have felt his
gospel to be the power of God, and the wisdom of
God; who have taken him for their only Lord and
King, and have given themselves unto him? Are
there so many of an opposite character—foolish,
mere nominal Christians, in the same state in which
they were born—who, whatever light you may have
in your heads, have no saving grace in your hearts?
And is the Bridegroom coming? Will He come
quickly,—come at an hour that ye think not? And
shall they that are ready enter in, and the door be
shut, and you stand without and cry for admittance,
but cry in vain? How dreadful the thought,—how
fearful the issue! I would be far, very far from

judging uncharitably of you; but I know the deceitfulness of the human heart. Surely they who propose to undertake an office, the design of which is to win souls, had need to be convinced, deeply convinced about their own souls."*

The most profound silence reigned while Mr Brown addressed the students in such strains. The language, the tone, the general manner, as well as the sentiments,—every circumstance, in short, was calculated to make a deep impression on their minds.

It was also a custom of Mr Brown, when any of his students were settled in the ministry, to write to them letters containing salutary counsels relative to the work in which they were now engaged ; and, on other occasions, he would also write letters to them in reference to their peculiar circumstances.† The following extract from one which he addressed to the Rev. Alexander Waugh, who had been lately settled over a small congregation in the village of Newtown, Roxburghshire, and who was afterwards translated to London, will show with what plainness and fidelity he wrote to them :—" I know the vanity of your heart, that you will feel mortified that your congregation is very small in comparison of

* Hay and Belfrage's Memoir of the Rev. Alexander Waugh, D.D., third edition, p. 36. The addresses here given were not taken from any MS. of Mr Brown's. They appear to have been reports of them written down probably by one of his students; but they are so much in character, that we have no doubt they are fairly given.

† Posthumous Works, p. 36.

those of your brethren around you ; but assure yourself, on the word of an old man, that when you come to give an account of them to the Lord Christ at his judgment-seat, you will think you have had enough." * These are solemn and weighty words, and may well check the ambition of aspiring minds.

To a minister who he understood was careless in his preparation for the pulpit, he addressed the following solemn warning:—" Think, as before God, my friend, that if you spend your devoted time— which ought to have been spent in religious reading, meditation, and prayer—in unnecessary sleep, in idle chat, or even reasonable conversation, in worldly business or recreation, or in reading of improper books, or even of proper books when it is not expedient;—if trusting to your own conceited or real abilities, or through sloth, you retail your raw, undigested thoughts, so as perhaps to render your sermons little better than a confused heap of truths, if not of trifles ; or frequently repeat your old discourses,—think, as before God, whether you can expect any other sentence than ' O thou wicked and slothful servant : bind him hand and foot, and cast him into outer darkness ; there shall be weeping, and wailing, and gnashing of teeth.' ' Cursed be he that doeth the work of the Lord deceitfully.' Alas ! shall I at the last day hear—shall I heartily join in the curses which shall be thus publicly poured forth against you by the Divine Persons whom you have treacherously affronted and betrayed ; by the angels

* Evangelical Magazine, 1805, p. 26.

whom you have provoked; by believers whom you
have grieved; and by the wicked multitudes whom
you have villanously damned by your sloth, and your
unconcern for the edification of souls?" * Would that
many ministers would lay these words to heart ! †

* United Presbyterian Magazine, 1850, p. 310.

† We feel so much the importance of diligence in study
as a qualification of ministers, that we cannot forbear quoting
here the following testimony of the Rev. Sydney Smith,—
a man whose opinion, considering the character of his own
mind (light, witty, yet sagacious), possesses peculiar weight
on such a subject :—

" The first thing to be done in conducting the understanding, is precisely the same as in conducting the body,—to
give it regular and copious supplies of food, to prevent that
atrophy and marasmus of mind which comes on from giving
it no new ideas. It is a mistake equally fatal to the memory,
the imagination, the powers of reasoning, and to every
faculty of the mind, to think too early that we can live
upon our stock of understanding,—that it is time to leave
off business, and make use of the acquisitions we have already made, without troubling ourselves any further to add
to them. It is no more possible for an idle man to keep together a certain stock of knowledge, than it is possible to
keep together a stock of ice exposed to the meridian sun.
Every day destroys a fact, a relation, or an inference; and
the only method of preserving the bulk and value of the
pile is by constantly adding to it.

" The prevailing idea with young people has been the in-
compatibility of labour and genius; and, therefore, from the
fear of being thought dull, they have thought it necessary
to remain ignorant. I have seen at school and at college a
great many young men completely destroyed by having
been so *un*fortunate as to produce an excellent copy of verses.
Their genius being now established, all that remained for

Among the works which he compiled with a special view to the improvement of those who had studied under him for the ministry, was " The Chris-

them to do was to act up to the dignity of the character; and as this dignity consisted in reading nothing new, in forgetting what they had already read, and in pretending to be acquainted with all subjects, by a sort of off-hand exertion of talents, they soon collapsed into the most frivolous and insignificant of men. . . . . There are many modes of being frivolous, and not a few of being useful; there is but one mode of being intellectually great,—and that is hard labour.

" It would be an extremely profitable thing to draw up a short and well-authenticated account of the habits of study of the most celebrated writers, with whose style of literary industry we happen to be most acquainted. It would go very far to destroy the absurd and pernicious association of genius and idleness, by showing them that the greatest poets, orators, statesmen, and historians—men of the most brilliant and imposing talents—have actually laboured as hard as the makers of dictionaries and the arrangers of indices; and that the most obvious reason why they have been superior to other men is, that they have taken more pains than other men. Gibbon was in his study every morning, winter and summer, at six o'clock; Mr Burke was the most laborious and indefatigable of human beings; Leibnitz was never out of his library; Pascal killed himself by study; Cicero narrowly escaped death by the same cause; Milton was at his books with as much regularity as a merchant or an attorney,—he had mastered all the knowledge of his time; so had Homer. Rafaelle lived but thirty-seven years, and in that short space carried his art so far beyond what it had before reached, that he appears to stand alone as a model to his successors. There are instances to the contrary; but, generally speaking, the life of all truly great men tian, the Student, and Pastor," exemplified in the lives of a number of excellent ministers in Scotland, England, and America. In the preface to this work,

has been a life of intense and incessant labour. They have commonly passed the first half of life in the gross darkness of indigent humility,—overlooked, mistaken, contemned by weaker men, thinking while others slept, reading while others rioted, feeling something within them that told them they should not always be kept down among the dregs of the world ; and then, when their time was come, and some little accident has given them their first occasion, they have burst out into the light and glory of public life, rich with the spoils of time, and mighty in all the labours and struggles of the mind. Then do the multitude cry out, ' A miracle of genius!' Yes, he *is* a miracle of genius, because he is a miracle of labour; because, instead of trusting to the resources of his own single mind, he has ransacked a thousand minds; because he makes use of the accumulated wisdom of ages, and takes as his point of departure the very last line and boundary to which science has advanced; because it has ever been the object of his life to assist every intellectual gift of nature, however munificent, and however splendid, with every resource that art could suggest, and every attention that diligence could bestow."—*Smith's Elementary Sketches of Moral Philosophy*, p. 96.

We recollect Dr Chalmers, in his first year's course as Professor of Divinity in the University of Edinburgh, in seeking to impress his pupils with the importance of diligence in study, told them not to wait for what might be considered as favourable times and seasons for study,—for an *afflatus*, as it is sometimes called,—but to sit down and pursue their studies doggedly at all times and at all seasons.

Though a man may have a few passable sermons on settling in the ministry, yet ere long his powers of preaching will come to be severely tried. To preach usefully and he thus writes : " To disparage the fashionable, but soul-ruining flimsiness in religion," which so much prevails, " and to promote a distinct, deep, and heart-

well, Sabbath after Sabbath, and month after month, and year after year, is no easy task, and will require the most assiduous study, and the vigorous exertion of all his faculties, in order that he may bring " out of his treasures things new and old,"—may " be a workman that needeth not to be ashamed, rightly dividing the word of life,"—and may at the last give in his account " with joy, and not with grief." *Hic labor; hoc opus.* It would be nothing short of a miracle if an idle, unstudious minister, were to be enabled to do this, —a miracle which God assuredly will never work. Such a man may well fear lest this should at last be his doom,— " Take ye the unprofitable servant, and cast him into outer darkness; there shall be weeping and gnashing of teeth." It is plain no man will so well deserve to perish as he who, having solemnly taken upon him the charge of the souls of others, has allowed them to perish for ever through his idleness and negligence. The late Mr Jay of Bath was a fine example of care and diligence in his preparations for the pulpit. To this he devoted the concentrated energies of his mind, and the result was seen in his admirable, useful preaching. This is, therefore, a subject on which he well deserves to be heard ; and the following is his testimony : " I have no idea," says he, " of a pastor who is not studious." " A man who has some degree of talent, especially an easiness and fluency of speech, may do for an itinerant or an occasional preacher, by his brisk superficialities ; but let him become stationary, and have to preach three or four times a-week to the same people, and he will soon abound with sameness, and become sapless and unedifying. The young will feel little attraction; the intelligent will be tempted to withdraw; the dull will become drowsy, and the ignorant who remain will be ignorant still."—*Jay's Autobiography*, p. 152.

captivating experience of the gracious working of the Spirit of God, issuing in a devout, active, and orderly practice, is the aim of the subsequent *Exemplification.* The shame, the pain, the pleasure which my own soul felt in abridging these lives, makes me hope that others may experience the like in reading them.

" Might I prevail with my pupils or others, I would earnestly obtest you for the Lord's sake, and for the sake of souls unnumbered, to lay *deep* the foundation of your professed religion, if you wish the *ravishing delights* of it. Formal gnawings of the shell will but render it disgustful to you, and make your ministrations of the gospel a task,—a burden to you, and a curse to your hearers. None that know how long and how eagerly I have hunted after human literature, as my circumstances permitted, will readily suspect me for an enthusiastic contemner of it. But as on the brink of eternity, I dare boldly pronounce it all 'vanity, and vexation of spirit,' when compared with, or not subordinate to the experimental knowledge of Jesus Christ, as ' made of God unto us wisdom, and righteousness, and sanctification, and redemption.' There is no *language,* ancient or modern, like that of the gospel of the grace of God, pronounced by the Holy Ghost to one's heart, and of heaven-born souls to God under his influence; no *history* like that of Jesus Christ, redemption through his blood, and effectual application of his grace ; no *science* like that of beholding the ' WORD made flesh,' and beholding the infinite

perfections of JEHOVAH in him, and through him, in
every creature,—as from eternity manifested, and to
be for ever manifested in our inconceivable happiness, 'to the praise of the glory of his grace;' no
pleasure like that of 'fellowship with the Father,
and with his Son Jesus Christ,' and all that joy
and peace with which the 'God of hope' fills men.
in believing,—that joy which is 'unspeakable, and
full of glory.' Come, then, 'let us go up to the
mountain of the God of Jacob, and he will teach us
of his ways, and we will walk in his paths. Come
ye, and let us walk in the light of the Lord.' Let
us be no more 'slothful, but followers of them who,
through faith and patience, inherit the promises.'"

In 1771 he lost his first wife, Mrs Janet Thomson,
daughter of Mr John Thomson, Musselburgh. He
had been married to her for about eighteen years,
and had several children by her, of whom two only
survived her, the one afterwards the Rev. John Brown
of Whitburn, the other the Rev. Ebenezer Brown of
Inverkeithing. Speaking of her death, he says, " I
confidently trust she went to her first and best husband." In a letter written to an aged friend about
this time, he also says, " I am the old man still, sin-
ning over the belly of troubles, convictions, and every
thing else. Only God can tell how inconsistent my
sermons and my inward life before God are; and
yet, after all, I cannot say he is a 'barren wilderness or land of drought.' Even yesterday he seemed
to smile, and enable my soul to say, Amen, to the last
clause of Zech. xiii. 9. In short my life is and has

been a kind of almost perpetual strife between God and my soul. He strives to overcome my enmity and wickedness with his mercies, and I strive to overcome his mercy with my enmity and wickedness. Astonishingly kind on his side, but worse than diabolically wicked on mine! After all, I wish and hope that he, not I, may obtain the victory at last. Time not allowing me to enlarge, I conclude, requesting your earnest prayers for me, and my congregation and students. One thing galls me with respect to my departed consort, that I did so little for the furtherance of her spiritual comfort and eternal salvation, and profited so little by her. Take heed, you and J——, and play not the fool as I did." Alas! in how many of our minds may these last words excite serious and solemn reflections!

Having thus mentioned some of the chief incidents in Mr Brown's life, we shall now notice a few of the more marked points in his character.

Mr Brown was a *Seceder* of the age in which he lived. He was but a boy when the Secession took place, and his mind was early and thoroughly imbued with its principles. Though he stedfastly avowed the principle that the Holy Scriptures are the only rule of faith and manners, yet, in common with the Seceders and others of his time, he was accustomed to make frequent reference to the acts of the Scottish Parliament, and to the acts of the General Assemblies of the Church of Scotland, particularly in what were held to be reforming times, to the Westminster Confession of Faith, and the Catechisms

Larger and Shorter, and to the sentiments of the leading Presbyterian ministers in Scotland, particularly in former times, as if they possessed weight and authority in matters of religion. He was particularly firm in his adherence to, and his zeal for the doctrine (then generally held by the professors of religion in Scotland), of the binding obligation of the National Covenant and of the Solemn League and Covenant on posterity. " These covenants," says he, " do and will, to all generations, bind ourselves and all the posterity of these covenanters, and of the societies which adopted them, to every duty engaged in them, and against every evil abjured, according as their stations, callings, and circumstances, require or admit. And as God, to whom these vows are made, is ruler everywhere on earth, no removal from Britain to another country, does, in the least, alter the obligation in any thing so far as he is concerned in it."* It is scarcely necessary to say that he was strongly opposed to the toleration of Popery in this country; but in this he was no way singular, for Scotland rose nearly as one man in opposition to the measures proposed for this end; and the mobs of London, lawless as they were, may be held as indications of the feelings very generally prevalent on the subject throughout England.†

* Posthumous Works, p. 105.

† Mr Brown, though a decided Seceder, was not blind to the faults and imperfections of the Secession. " I look, says he, in an address to his students, " I look upon the Secession as indeed the cause of God, but sadly mismanaged and dis-

He was remarkable for his *diligence* in study. As his congregation, though respectable for the character of its members, was not numerous, it allowed him to follow in this respect the natural bent of his mind. He was never more in his element than when in his study, and here he spent the greater part of his time. He was an early riser. In summer he used to rise between four and five in the morning, and in winter at six. From the time he rose he usually continued, except during the intervals of meals and family worship, in close study till eight o'clock in the evening. Formal visits he disliked exceedingly, and often said he would rather write a sermon than spend an hour in them. His people knew his disposition in this respect, and seldom invited him out, or called upon him unless on some important or useful errand.*

honoured by myself and others. Alas! for that pride, passion, selfishness, and unconcern for the glory of Christ and spiritual edification of souls, which has so often prevailed. Alas! for our want of due meekness, gentleness, holy zeal, self-denial, hearty grief for sin, compassion to souls in immediate connection with us, or left in the Established Church, which became distinguished witnesses for Christ. Alas! that we did not *chiefly* strive to pray better, preach better, and live better, than our neighbours."—*Brown's Compendious View of Natural and Revealed Religion*, p. xvi. Well were it for most churches if they were not so blind to their own faults and imperfections. This might save them from many evils, and perhaps lead both ministers and people to higher attainments, greater piety, and more usefulness.

* Posthumous Works, p. 28.

F

As a *preacher* Mr Brown was distinguished by
great plainness, faithfulness, seriousness, and earnestness. His learning he never brought into the pulpit,
unless by bringing down the great truths of religion
to the level of common capacities. He was much of
the mind of Archbishop Ussher, as expressed in that
golden saying,—" It will take all our learning to
make things plain." The Rev. Robert Simpson,
afterwards theological tutor of Hoxton Academy,
London, who, about the year 1770, heard him for
some time in his own meeting-house at Haddington,
made the following statement regarding his preaching:—" I well remember a searching sermon he
preached from these words, ' What went ye out for
to see?' &c. Although at that time I had no experimental acquaintance with the truth as it is in Jesus,
yet his grave appearance in the pulpit, his solemn,
weighty, and energetic manner of speaking, used to
affect me very much. Certainly his preaching was
close, and his address to the conscience pungent.
Like his Lord and Master he spoke with authority
and hallowed pathos, having tasted the sweetness and
felt the power of what he delivered." He was not
one of those preachers whose sermons were chiefly
taken up in cold statements as to the doctrines and
duties of religion. These he did not neglect, but he
ever brought them home to his hearers by earnest
and close application to their consciences and hearts.
Perhaps there was no part of his preaching so powerful and so heart-touching as his expostulations with
the unconverted.* Probably few men have come

* Posthumous Works, p. 30.

nearer than Mr Brown to Richard Baxter's style of preaching, as described by him in these memorable lines,—

> " I preach'd as never sure to preach again;
> And as a dying man to dying men." *

Oh for a host of such preachers! †

Mr Brown's delivery was strongly characterised by that *sing-song* which prevailed much in the Secession especially in his early days; and though all departures from a natural delivery are greatly to be deprecated, yet this in him was singularly melting to serious minds. I can have no recollection of his delivery myself, but I have heard it imitated by my brother Ebenezer, and I felt it so touching and overpowering that I question if the highest flights of oratory would

* Poetical Fragments of Richard Baxter, p. 35.

† We were told by an aged minister, who had been one of his students, that he once said to him, " Mr Brown, you are often speaking against Richard Baxter, but I see no man so like Richard Baxter as yourself." The compliment was high, yet it was not undeserved. In what we have said, we do not mean to place him on a level with Baxter in point of genius, imagination, invention; or of rich, felicitous, powerful expression: we refer chiefly to the earnest and melting appeals which both were in the habit of making to the hearts and consciences of their hearers, particularly of the unconverted. The above-mentioned lines of Baxter we were accustomed to quote as expressive of a resolution on his part; but on lately turning to the poem from which they are taken, we found they expressed not simply his resolution, but his practice in the early period of his life, when his ill health gave him a " frequent sight of death," and made him " live as in the sight of heaven and hell."

have had any thing like the same impression on my mind.*

It was his usual practice, both before and after he came from public worship, to retire to his closet and pour out his heart to God in prayer. Trifling conversation at any time, and especially after being engaged in the solemnities of divine worship, he particularly detested. †

The personal religion of Mr Brown was of a high

---

* A *sing-song* delivery was not peculiar to the early Secession, or other Presbyterian ministers. It has prevailed extensively in religious services. Mrs Stowe, the author of " Uncle Tom's Cabin," after attending the yearly meeting of the female Quakers in London, makes the following remarks: " There are some things in the mode of speaking among Friends, particularly in their public meetings, which do not strike me agreeably, and to which I think it would take me some time to become accustomed, such as a kind of *intoning*, somewhat similar to the manner in which the Church service is performed in cathedrals. It is a curious fact that religious exercises, in all ages and countries, have inclined to this form of expression. It appears in the cantilation of the synagogue, the service of the cathedral, the prayers of the Covenanters and the Puritans."—*Mrs Stowe's Sunny Memories of Foreign Lands*, vol. ii. p. 79.

The only Chinese we ever heard read, read with a sing-song, similar to that which formerly prevailed in the Secession.

In the Memoir of the Rev. Dr Waugh of London, we find the following statement regarding my father:—" Dr Waugh used to mention the following anecdote of his venerable instructor, which had occurred within his own knowledge.

† Posthumous Works, p. 31.

order. He was characterised by deep, serious, earnest piety. He was remarkable for a powerful sense of his own sinfulness, especially of sins of the heart. Many will perhaps wonder at the language which he often employs on this subject. Having no such feelings themselves, they may be apt to think it very extreme, but he had a more than ordinary lively sense of the strictness and spirituality of the divine law, and he saw how much he fell short, both in heart and life, of its requirements. His deep sense of his sinful-

It happened that at some public solemnity, where the celebrated David Hume was one of the audience, Mr Brown was preceded by an ambitious young man, who delivered a very eloquent and florid address, the old divine following in one equally remarkable for its simplicity and earnestness. 'The first preacher,' said the sceptic to one of his friends, ' spoke as if he did not believe what he said; the latter as if he was conscious that the Son of God stood at his elbow.' "—*Hay and Belfrage's Memoir of the late Alexander Waugh, D.D.*, p. 51.

On what authority this story *originally* rested we are not here told, and unless it was supported by good evidence, I would be little disposed to believe it. It is scarcely very likely that Mr Hume ever heard my father preach, and perhaps still less likely that he would express such an opinion of his delivery and in such phraseology. In drawing up this memoir, I originally omitted any reference to this story; but finding that it has got into the new edition of the " Encyclopædia Britannica," now publishing, in a biographical notice of my father, and as this may henceforth come to be held as authority for it, I think it right to take this notice of it. That such a story, however, should have arisen, is perhaps some indication of the truth of the account I have given of the earnestness and impressiveness of his preaching.

ness led him to give a cordial acceptance to the salvation of Christ as freely offered in the Gospel. Salvation by grace was a doctrine peculiarly precious to his soul, and it was his special delight to preach it to others. He felt that were it not for the rich, free, sovereign grace of God, neither he nor any other sinner of the human family could hope to be saved. He appears during the greater part of his life to have enjoyed a comfortable hope of his interest in Christ, and of " the glory which shall be revealed." On this subject he holds undoubting language—we recollect of no instance of his giving utterance to doubts or fears. He was little taken up about the world or worldly matters, but appears to have lived very much under the influence of spiritual and eternal things. The holy breathings of his soul may be seen in many of his writings.

We cannot but here notice particularly his strict observation of the Lord's day. This was a marked feature in his character. He had none of those lax notions in regard to Sabbath sanctification, which prevail so much in the present day not only among men of the world but among many professors of religion. He was never able to bring himself to believe that nine out of the ten commandments, given by God to Moses on Mount Sinai, with so much solemnity, were of moral and permanent obligation ; but that the other—that in reference to the Sabbath— was little better than a mere Judaical institution, and that its observation under the Christian dispensation was little more than a matter of expediency, and that man might cut and carve upon it just as suited his dispositions or convenience. Though he would no doubt admit that there were precepts in the laws of Moses in reference to the Sabbath, which had a special reference to the Israelites, just as there were precepts in reference to some other parts of the Decalogue, which were peculiar to them, yet he did not consider that these affected the substance and spirit of the commandments themselves as given on Mount Sinai.*

With him the observation of the Sabbath did not consist in mere outward forms, or simply in attendance on public worship; the private and family exercises of religion were, in his estimation, of no less importance and not less essential to its right observance. Such passages as Isaiah lviii. 13, 14, " If thou turn away thy foot from the Sabbath, from doing thy pleasure on my holy day; and call the Sabbath a delight, the holy of the Lord, honourable; and shall honour him, not doing thine own ways, nor finding thine own pleasure, nor speaking thine own words: then shalt thou delight thyself in the Lord," &c.; and

* Among the Israelites the punishment of death was inflicted for certain breaches of the *First* Commandment, Deut. xiii. 1–18; of the *Second* Commandment, Deut. xvii. 2–7; of the *Third* Commandment, Lev. xxiv. 10–16; of the *Fifth* Commandment, Lev. xxi. 9, Deut. xxi. 18–21; of the *Seventh* Commandment, Lev. xx. 10–14, Deut xxii. 22–27; but no one can conclude from these special enactments that the original commandments themselves were merely Judaical institutions and are now no longer in force.

Rev. i. 10, " I was in the Spirit on the Lord's day," (understanding these words as expressive of a spiritual state of mind), he considered as showing the manner in which the Sabbath should still be observed. To talk of worldly matters, of the public news, or common occurrences, or even of the external affairs of the Church, he considered sinful; and as he would not allow himself in saying or doing what he deemed inconsistent with Sabbath sanctification, he endeavoured to restrain all within his house from such practices.* His views and practice in regard to the Sabbath were of a truly spiritual nature, and while we are persuaded of their scripturalness, they have also the recommendation of consistency throughout. Unless we draw a strong and marked line of demarcation between the Sabbath and the other six days of the week,—such a line as is drawn in the Fourth Commandment,—we shall find it difficult, if not impossible, to draw any line at all. If, for example, we may talk of worldly matters, or of common news, why may we not read the newspapers? And if the newspapers, why not history, ancient or modern, civil or ecclesiastical? And if history, why not works in philosophy or works of imagination? In short, why not in the whole range of science and literature? —thus destroying all distinction between the Sabbath and the other days of the week. Of the importance and value of the Sabbath, he had a deep yet not too strong a conviction. Though the outward observance of it is no proof of inward piety, either

* Posthumous Works, p. 27.

in a nation or an individual, yet it is favourable to the production and cultivation of inward piety; while on the other hand the neglect of the Sabbath, if not a proof of the absolute want of piety in a nation or an individual, will generally be found to be an indication of a low state of piety, and will certainly lead to its still further decline. Of this, the state of religion among the nations of the continent, Protestant as well as Popish, is a melancholy example.

In charity he was exemplary. His salary from his congregation was but small. For a considerable time it was only £40 a-year, and it never exceeded £50. As professor of divinity he received no salary at all. He had, we believe, some other sources of income, but we have no reason to think they were considerable. With what he possessed it was his aim to do good, as far as lay in his power, especially to the household of faith. It was his opinion that every man is bound to devote at least a tenth of his income to pious and charitable purposes; and though he had a numerous family he often exceeded this proportion. He exercised a frugality in his expenses upon his own person, which some of his brethren thought was extreme. It appeared, however, that his sole design in denying himself some of the conveniences or comforts of life was, that he might be the more able to supply the necessities of others. When he had opportunity he commonly accompanied his alms with good advice, that while the body was supplied the soul might be saved. To poor congregations who wished a collection from his people, as they were few and generally poor, he several times sent considerable sums out of his own pocket, and he frequently caused " the heart of the widow to sing for joy." Disgusted with ostentation in others, the alms which he himself gave were so secretly distributed, that they were seldom known except by those who partook of his liberality.*

In conversation it was apparent to all that his constant aim was to inform and edify. He seldom gave any opinion on politics or intermeddled with them. The remarks which he made when others introduced subjects of that kind, were generally of a religious nature. Instead of expressing approbation, or passing censure on the conduct of our rulers, he used to take notice of that Providence which manageth all things for the glory of God and the good of his Church. To talk in company about the increase of ministers' salaries, he studiously avoided, as knowing well that " they who minister at the altar," lie too often under the odium of mercenariness, and that nothing has a greater tendency to hinder the edification of the people than a suspicion that their minister preaches for worldly gain. Concerning the proceedings of church courts he seldom said any thing to private Christians; and when any of his members were chargeable with improper conduct, he carefully concealed it. He could not see how relating such things could promote the spiritual interests of his people. †

Through a stedfast faith in the divine promises, he appeared to have attained an habitual evenness of

* Posthumous Works, p. 29.   † Ibid. p. 27.

mind; never being much transported with joy, nor much depressed with sorrow. In him the promise was remarkably fulfilled,—" Thou wilt keep him in perfect peace whose mind is stayed on thee, because he trusteth in thee." On one occasion hearing a tremendous peal of thunder, he said to a friend very composedly, " That's the low whisper of my God." *

Much study, combined with a temper naturally serious, gave a gravity to his manners which those who were little acquainted with him were apt to mistake for severity. But though grave he was not gloomy. Among his friends he was agreeable and cheerful. His conversation abounded with religious anecdote, and was at times enlivened with innocent pleasantry. But in general it was more distinguished for its solidity than its brilliancy; its seriousness than its humour. After all, however, there probably was an undue degree of severity in some of his religious views, and in his own character as formed by them; a circumstance which is always to be deeply regretted when it is associated with true piety, as presenting religion under a forbidding aspect to others, and especially to the young.

Between the two branches of the Secession there was long little friendly feeling. Some of those who had taken part in the original proceedings, which led to the *breach*, were not yet off the stage of life, and they had been but too successful in imbuing the minds of their followers with their own unhallowed spirit. Though Mr Brown early took his side, we

* Posthumous Works, p. 28.

never find him manifesting unchristian feelings toward the opposite party. In a letter which he wrote not long before his death to the Rev. Archibald Bruce, of Whitburn, the respected professor of divinity of the Antiburgher body, he thus expressed himself: " Our conduct on both sides of the Secession I have often thought to be like that of two travellers, both walking on the same road, not far from one another, but in consequence of a thick mist suddenly come on they cannot see one another, and each supposes the other to be off the road. After some time the darkness is removed, and they are quite surprised to find that they are both on the road, and had been all along so near one another."*

The following solemn dedication of himself to the Lord, written about three years before his death, will furnish a striking illustration of some of the features in his character which we have already noticed :—

" HADDINGTON, *June* 23, 1784.

" Lord! I am now entering on the thirty-fourth year of my ministry,—an amazing instance of sovereign mercy and patience to a cumberer of the ground! How strange that thou shouldest have, for more than sixty years, continued striving to exercise mercy and loving-kindness upon a wretch, that hath all along spoken and done all the evil that I could ; nor ever would yield, but when the almighty influence of free grace put it out of my power to oppose it. Lord !

* Christian Repository, 1819, p. 610.

how often have I vowed, but never grown better;
confessed, but never amended! Often thou hast challenged and corrected me, and yet I have ' gone on
frowardly in the way of my heart.' As an ' evil man
and seducer,' I have grown worse and worse. But
where should a sinner flee but to the Saviour? Lord!
all refuge faileth me,—no man can help my soul.
Nothing will do for me, but an uncommon stretch of
thy Almighty grace. To thee, O Jesus! I give up
myself, as a foolish, guilty, polluted, and enslaved
sinner,—and I hereby solemnly take thee as mine, as
' made of God to me wisdom, righteousness, sanctification, and redemption.' I give up myself as a poor,
ignorant, careless, and wicked creature, who hath
been ' ever learning, and yet never able to come to
the knowledge of the truth,'—to thee, O Lord, that
thou mayest bestow gifts on the rebellious, and exalt
thy grace, in showing kindness to the unworthy. O
Saviour! come down, and do something for me before I die. I give up myself and family, wife,
children, and servant, to thee, encouraged by thy
promises, Gen. xvii. 7; Jer. xxxi. 1; Isa. xliv. 3,
lix. 21. I commit my poor, weak, withered congregation, deprived by death of its pillars, that thou
mayest strengthen, refresh, and govern it. I commit
all my students unto thee, that thou, O Lord, mayest
train them up for the ministry. May never one of
them be so unfit as I have been! Lord! I desire to
take hold of thy new ' covenant, well ordered in all
things and sure. This is all my salvation and all
my desire.'   JOHN BROWN."

The following address to his congregation, and other hearers, written in the view of death, also strikingly illustrates many features in his character, particularly as a minister :—

" MY DEAR HEARERS, — Having, through the patience and mercy of God, long laboured among you, not as I ought,—far, very far from it,—but as I could, I must now leave you, to appear before the judgment-seat of Christ, to give an account of my stewardship. You cannot say that I ever appeared to covet any ' man's silver or gold, or apparel,' or ever uttered one murmur about what you gave me ; or that I sought yours, not you. You cannot charge me with idling away my devoted time in vain chat, either with you or others, or with spending it in worldly business, reading of plays, romances, or the like. If I had, what an awful appearance should I soon have before my all-seeing Judge! You cannot pretend that I spared either body or mind in the service of your souls, or that I put you off with airy conceits of man's wisdom, or any thing else than the truths of God. Though I was not ashamed, as I thought Providence called me, to give you hints of the truths presently injured, and the support of which is the declared end of the Secession, yet I laboured chiefly to show and inculcate upon your consciences the most important truths concerning your sinfulness and misery, and the way of salvation from both through Christ, and laboured to hunt you out of all your lying refuges, and give your consciences no rest but in Christ and him crucified. The delight of my soul was to commend him and his free and great salvation to your souls, and to direct and encourage you to receive and walk in him. ' I call heaven and earth to record against you this day, that I laboured to set life and death, blessing and cursing, before you, and to persuade you to choose life that ye might live.' By the grace of God I have endeavoured, however poorly, to live holily, justly, and unblameably, among you. And now I leave all these discourses, exhortations, instructions, and examples, as a testimony for the Lord against you, if you lay not your eternal salvation to heart as ' the one thing needful, that good part which shall not be taken from you.'

" But I have no confidence in any of these things before God as my Judge. I see such weakness, such deficiency, such unfaithfulness, such imprudence, such unfervency and unconcern, such selfishness, in all that I have done as a minister or a Christian, as richly deserves the deepest damnation of hell. I have no hope of eternal happiness but in Jesus' blood, which cleanseth from all sin,—in ' redemption through his blood, the forgiveness of my sins, according to the riches of his grace.' It is the everlasting covenant of God's free grace, well ' ordered in all things and sure, that is all my salvation and all my desire.'

" Now I die firmly persuaded of the truth of those things which I preached unto you. I never preached unto you any other way of salvation than I essayed to use for myself. I now, when dying, ' set to my seal that God is true.' After all that I have said of

the sinfulness of your hearts, I have not represented
to you the ten thousandth part of their vileness and
guilt. Knowing, in some measure, ' the terror of
the Lord,' I endeavoured to persuade you, that it is
a fearful thing to fall into the hands of his wrath:
but ' who knoweth the power of his anger?' Knowing, in some measure, the deceitfulness of sin, and
the devices of Satan, I laboured to warn you of them.
But what especially delighted my heart was, to set
before you the excellencies, the love, the labours of
our Redeemer, and God in him, giving himself, and
applying himself to sinful men; and to represent to
you the work of God on the heart ' in the day of his
power,' and the exercise of the heart in its diversified
frames. What I saw, and tasted, and handled, both
of the bitter and the sweet in religion, I delivered
unto you. Little as I am acquainted with the Lord,
I will leave it as my dying testimony, that there is
none like Christ,—there is nothing like fellowship
with Christ. I dare aver before God, angels and
men, that I would not exchange the pleasures of
religion which I have enjoyed, especially in the days
of my youth, for all the pleasures, profits, and honours
of this world, since the creation till the present moment, ten thousand times told. For what then would
I exchange my entrance ' into the joy of my Lord,'
and being for ever with him? Truly God hath been
good to a soul that but poorly sought him. Oh!
what would he be to yours, if you would earnestly
seek him! With what heart-ravishing power and
grace hath he testified against my wicked and unbe-

lieving heart, that ' he is God, even my God !' And now, ' whom have I in heaven but him ? nor is there any on earth whom I desire besides him. My heart and flesh fail, but God is the strength of my heart and my portion for ever.' Left early by both father and mother, God hath taken me up, and been the orphan's stay. He hath ' given me the heritage of those that fear him.' ' The lines have fallen to me in pleasant places. I have a goodly heritage. The Lord is the portion of mine inheritance and of my cup,—he maintaineth my lot:' ' Yea, mine own God is he,—my God that doth me save.'

" Had I ten thousand worlds in my offer, and these secured to me for ever, they should be utterly contemned. ' Doubtless I count all things but loss for the excellency of the knowledge of Christ Jesus my Lord; and I do count them but dung that I may win him, and be found in him, not having mine own righteousness, which is of the law, but the righteousness which is of God through faith.'

" Now, when I go to give my account to God, think what it must be! Alas! must it be, that in too great conformity to your careless neighbours, some did not attend the means of grace at examinations,* meetings for prayer and spiritual conference, as ye ought? Must it be, that after labouring so many years among you, I left less lively religion in the congregation than I found in it at first? Must it be, that ye were called, but ye made light of the marriage with Christ, and of his great salvation? Must it be,

* See p. 34.

G

that ye contented yourselves with a form of godliness, without knowing the power of it? Must it be, that some few, trampling on their most solemn engagements, forsook me, 'having loved this present world?' Must it be, that others were not careful to train up their seed for the Lord? Must it be, that ye often heard the most searching sermons, or the most delightful, and went away quite unaffected? Or must it be, that ye were awakened, that your souls looked to Jesus and were enlightened; that ye believed with your heart unto salvation; that ye harrowed in the seed of the truth, which I sowed among you, by serious meditation and fervent prayer; that ye laboured to win souls to Christ? Alas! I fear many of you will go down to hell with a lie in your right hand,—go down to hell with all the gospel sermons and exhortations you ever heard in your conscience, to assist it to upbraid, gnaw, and torment you! My dearly beloved hearers, shall I see you next, at the last day, standing at the left hand of your Judge? Shall I see those faces all in flames, and those eyes which often looked at me, looking lively bright horror at the judgment-seat of Christ? Must I hear the Redeemer pronounce on you that awful sentence, ' Depart from me, ye cursed, into everlasting fire, prepared for the devil and his angels'? And must I, who have so often prayed for your salvation, and preached for your salvation, add my hearty Amen to the sentence of your eternal damnation? God forbid!

"Let me then beseech you now, without a moment's delay, to consider your ways. Oh! listen to the Lord's invitations! Believe his self-giving declarations and promises, which, times without number, have, with some measure of earnestness, been sounded in your ears! For the Lord's sake dare not, at your infinite peril, to see me again in your sins, and refusers of my glorious Redeemer and Master! Oh! give him your hearts,—give him your hearts! I never complained of your giving me too little. Nay, I thought myself happier than most of my brethren as to all outward matters. But I always thought and complained that you did not use my master Christ as I wished, in your hearts, lives, and houses. And now I ask nothing for myself, or any of my family, but make this my dying request, that you would now receive my master Christ into your hearts and houses. Could my soul speak back to you from the eternal state,— could all my rotting bones and sinews, and every bit of my body, speak back to you from the grave,—they should all cry, ' Oh that ye were wise, that ye understood this, that ye would consider your latter end! Oh that ye would give my master Christ these ignorant, guilty, polluted, and enslaved hearts of yours, that he, as " made of God unto you wisdom, righteousness, and sanctification, and redemption," might enter in and fill them for ever with his grace and truth! Oh, say not to a dying, a dead minister —rather, oh, say not to a living Redeemer, and to his Father, and to his blessed Spirit—Nay.'

" Dearly beloved, whom I wish to be ' my joy and crown' in the day of the Lord, suffer me to speak from the dead to you. Let me exhort you, by all your inexpressible sinfulness and misery,—by all the perfections, words, and works of God,—by all the excellencies, offices, relations, labours, sufferings, glory, and fulness of Christ,—by all the joys of heaven and the horrors of hell,—now to make serious work of the eternal salvation of your souls. Try what improvement you have made of all my ministrations. Call to mind what of my texts, sermons, or other instructions, you can; and pray them over before the Lord, applying them closely to your own conscience and heart. Wash yourselves thoroughly, in the blood of Jesus Christ, from all the sins of holy things since you and I met together.

" I recommend to you, young persons, my two addresses annexed to my Catechisms; and to you, parents and masters, my address in the 'Awakening Call,' and my sermons on 'Raising up children to Christ,' as a part of my dying words to you. They will rise up in judgment against you, if you contemn them.

" With respect to your obtaining another minister, let me beseech you, by much fervent prayer, to get him first from the Lord. And let it be your care to call one whose sermons you find to touch your consciences. May the Lord preserve you from such as aim chiefly to tickle your fancy, and seek themselves rather than Jesus Christ the Lord! Let there be no strife among you in calling him. And when you get him, labour at his entrance to receive his message from Christ with great greediness. Let your vacancy make you hungry and thirsty for the gospel. And let all hands and hearts be intent on raising up a seed for Christ in poor withered and wicked East Lothian.

" Oh! how it would delight my soul to be informed, in the manner of the eternal state, that Christ had come along with my successor, ' conquering and to conquer!' How gladly should I see you and him by hundreds at the right hand of Christ at the great day, though I should scarcely have my ten! Oh, if Christ were so exalted, so remembered among you, as to make me scarcely thought of! I desire to decrease, that he may increase.

" Now ' unto Him that loved us, and washed us from our sins in his blood,' and ' hath given us everlasting consolation and good hope through grace,' be honour and glory, dominion and blessing, for ever and ever.

" ' This is a faithful saying, and worthy of all acceptation, that Christ Jesus came into the world to save sinners, of whom I am the chief.'—Your once affectionate pastor,

" JOHN BROWN."

Happy, happy, happy the minister who, at the close of a pastorship of thirty or forty years, can with truth thus address the people of his charge!

For some years before his death, Mr Brown laboured under stomach complaints, the result probably of his studious habits. In the beginning of 1787 his disease greatly increased. His friends observed it with grief, and wished him to desist from part of his public work, but he said to them in reply, " I am determined to hold to Christ's work so long as I can. How can a dying man spend his last breath better than in preaching Christ?" On the 25th of February,

which was his last Sabbath in the pulpit, he preached
from Luke ii. 26, " It was revealed unto him by the
Holy Ghost, that he should not see death, before he
had seen the Lord's Christ." In the close of his sermon,
he took a solemn farewell of his own congregation,
and plainly intimated that in the pulpit they would
see his face no more. Though he was now scarcely
able to support himself, he preached the usual evening sermon, and seemed to preach with more earnestness than ever. This, his last sermon, was from Acts
xiii. 26, " To you is the word of this salvation sent."
As in the afternoon he had addressed the people more
immediately under his pastoral charge, in the evening he, in a very affecting manner, bade adieu to his
hearers, mostly members of the Established Church.

About the very time that he retired from his public work as a minister, a letter was addressed to him
by the Rev. Charles Simeon of Cambridge, an excellent minister of the Church of England, which
could not fail to be highly gratifying to him, as
opening a new prospect of the usefulness of his
writings, particularly of his Self-interpreting Bible.
The Rev. Mr Caius, the biographer of Mr Simeon,
gives us the following account:—" The copy of the
Scriptures which became the favourite companion of
his devotional hours from this period, was a quarto
volume of Brown's Self-interpreting Bible, which, to
the end of his life, he was continually enriching with
valuable notes of his own. So much did he prize
this commentary, that in 1787, January 19th, he
wrote to the author at Haddington: ' Your Self-

interpreting Bible seems to stand in lieu of all other comments; and I am daily receiving so much edification and instruction from it, that I would wish it in the hands of all serious ministers. I have conceived a thought of purchasing a few to give to those godly ministers who would find it very inconvenient to purchase it for themselves. But having no very great affluence myself, it is necessary that I should proceed on the most saving plan. I take the liberty, therefore, of asking whether you (whose heart seems to be much set upon forwarding the cause of Christ) could procure me forty copies at the booksellers' price for that purpose alone, and to inform me whether there will be a new edition soon.' " * What answer Mr Brown returned to this benevolent proposal of Mr Simeon, we do not know; we rather suppose the work was then out of print.

Mr Brown had been little given, through life, to speak of his own religious experience. He was even reserved in giving utterance to his religious feelings, and especially to such feelings as might in any way ·be interpreted as reflecting honour on himself. But when he came to die, he opened his heart very freely, and breathed forth many holy sentiments and aspirations, which are the more satisfactory, as they were in such perfect harmony with his life. The following notes of his dying sayings were taken down in writing by his son, the Rev. Ebenezer Brown of Inverkeithing, almost as they fell from his lips; but as he had to attend to his ministerial duties in a part of

* Caius' Memoir of the Rev. Charles Simeon, p. 67.

the country at some distance, much of what he said
in his absence was forgotten :—

March 2.—A friend observing that he ought to
be more careful in the use of means for his recovery,
he replied, " If Christ be magnified, whether in my
life or death, that is the great matter."

March 3.—One happening to talk in his presence
about reading history, he remarked, " Often we read
history as Atheists or Deists, rather than as Christians. To read of events without observing the hand
of God in them, is to read as Atheists: to read and
not observe how all events conduce to carry on the
work of redemption, is to read as Deists." In the
evening, his spirits being apparently sunk, and his
relations taking notice of it, he said, " A piece of
history hath sometimes amused me when my natural
spirits were low ; but now I find no pleasure except
in meditating on the promises : I wish to begin with
that in Genesis, ' The seed of the woman shall bruise
the head of the serpent,' and to delight myself with
it, and all the rest that follow, to the end of the Re-
velation of John."

March 4.—An acquaintance saying to him, that
it was pleasant to see the excellent Mr Hervey
insisting so much on grace reigning through righteousness : " Yes," replied he, " that is the doctrine
which it is good to live with, and good to die with."

This being Sabbath, he went out to hear a sermon. After returning to his house, he said, " Oh!
what a happy life might a Christian have, if he were

always persuaded of the love of God which is in Christ Jesus our Lord! If there were such a thing as exchange of learning, I would willingly quit with all my acquaintance with languages, &c., to know, experimentally, what that meaneth, 'I am crucified with Christ: nevertheless I live; yet not I, but Christ liveth in me; and the life which I now live in the flesh, I live by the faith of the Son of God, who loved me, and gave himself for me.' "

In the evening, being asked if he thought himself better, he answered, with a great deal of composure, " I am no worse: but I do not wish to have a will in that matter; only I would not desire to live, and yet not be able for Christ's work,—though perhaps, were God so ordering it, he would enable me to bear that too."

March 6.—He called his two eldest sons, the Revs. John and Ebenezer Brown, into his room; and, as they were about to leave him for a time, he exhorted them, in the most earnest manner, to trust in the Lord, and to be doing good. " No doubt," said he, " I have met with trials as well as others; yet so kind hath God been to me, that I think, if God were to give me as many years as I have already lived in the world, I would not desire one single circumstance in my lot changed,—except that I wish I had less sin."

March 20.—He had now become much weaker than he was before. His memory was much impaired, but his judgment was as entire as ever. He conversed like a man who quite overlooked earthly things, and seemed to have his affections almost

wholly set on things above. Some of his expressions
were as follows :—

" I have often wondered at the favour which men
have shown to me, but much more at the favour of
God to such a grievous sinner."

"Oh! to be with God, to 'see him as he is,—to know
him even as I am known ;' it is worthy, not merely
of going for, but of dying for, to see a smiling God."

" About the year ——, God said to my soul, ' I
have loved thee with an everlasting love ;' and, oh!
how faithful hath he been to that since ! "

" There would not have been more grace shown
in the redemption of the chief of devils, than in saving me ; the same price would have ransomed them,
—the same strivings would have overcome them."

" Men may talk of the sovereignty of redeeming
love as they will ; but had it not been sovereign, infinitely sovereign, I had as surely been damned as if
I were in hell already."

" Were it not that God foresaw our sins and provocations from eternity, he never could have continued his love to me, the grievous sinner,—the
arrant rebel ; yet I think he is now preparing me
for being ever with himself. Oh! what is that! I
have done all that lies in my power to damn myself,
and though I will not say that God hath done all
that he could to save me, yet I am sure he hath done
a great deal."

" If angels and men knew the raging enmity of
my heart, what would they think of redeeming love,
which hath pitched on me ! "

" Oh! what a miracle to see me, the arrant rebel, sitting on the throne with Jesus! And I hope I shall be seen there. What cannot Jesus do!"

" Oh! how these words, ' He loved ME, and gave himself for ME,' once penetrated into my heart, and made me cry, ' Bless the Lord, O my soul, and let all that is within me be stirred up to bless his holy name.' "

A friend asking him if he had any appetite for his supper, he replied, " Yes: oh! if I had but as good an appetite for the fulness of God, as I have for earthly victuals!"

One remarking to him, that under all his weakness, his mind seemed to be very composed, he answered, " Indeed I am composed; God hath put a bridle in my mouth; and though I have been a most perverse wretch, yet he hath strangely restrained me; and oh! how amazing! he hath done this chiefly by loving-kindnesses and tender mercies; and is not that a strange bridle for such an imp of hell as I have been?"

" I cannot say that I have found God's words and eaten them; but truly his words have found me, and have been given me, and have been to me the joy and rejoicing of my heart."

" Oh! that is a sweet little sentence, ' We shall be for ever with the Lord!' Oh, how sweet!—FOR EVER with the LORD! And that which makes the wonder is this, that it is WE that are to enjoy this happiness;—WE pitiful wretches are to be for ever with God our Saviour,—God in our nature!"

" How amazing the mystery of redemption, in which the rich deservants of hell are exalted to the throne of God, and that by the blood of our Lord Jesus Christ ! "

" Oh ! to be brought to this point,

> Then will I to God's altar go,
>   To God MY chiefest joy :
> Yea, God, MY God, thy name to praise
>   My harp I will employ.
>
> PSALM xliii. 4.—*Scotch Metrical Version.*

" I ' desire to depart and to be with Christ, which is far better : ' and though I have lived sixty years very comfortably in this world, yet I would gladly turn my back on you all, to be with Christ. I am sure Christ may say of me, ' These sixty years this wretch hath grieved me.' "

March 21.—In the preceding evening when he fell asleep, he seemingly left his heart with Christ ; and if we may guess the subject of his thoughts by his words this morning when he awoke, he was still with him. Among the first words he uttered, were these : " Oh ! it is pleasant to enjoy fellowship with Christ. Any small acquaintance I have had of him convinceth me of this. And, oh ! how much more pleasure might I have had, had it not been for my own folly and wickedness ! I think that I could now willingly die to see HIM, who is ' white and ruddy, the chiefest among ten thousand.' "

When at breakfast, he expressed himself thus : " How amazing that a rich deservant of hell should get such a meal! how much more that a rich deservant of hell should get such a Christ!"

Addressing himself to his two sons in the ministry, he said, with peculiar earnestness, "Oh! labour, labour for Christ while ye have strength. I now repent that I have been so lazy and so slothful in his service. Oh! commend Jesus. I have been looking at him for these many years, and never yet could find a fault in him, but what was of my own making; though he hath seen ten thousand thousand faults in me. Many a comely person I have seen, but none so comely as Christ; many a kind friend I have had, but none like Christ in loving-kindnesses and tender mercies."

Some short time after, he said to them, "I know not whether I shall ever see you together again or not; but oh! labour, labour to win souls to Christ; —there is none like Christ,—there is none like Christ,—there is none like Christ! I am sure a poor worthless wretch he hath had of me; but a precious, superlatively precious Christ I have had of him. Never grudge either purse or person for Christ; I can say this, that I never was a loser by any time spent, or by any money given for him."

"Oh the pains which God hath been at to save me, and the pains which I had been at to destroy myself! But he hath partly gained, and I hope that he will completely gain the victory."

After taking a ride in a chaise, when he came into his house, he remarked, "Reading tires me, walking tires me, riding tires me; but, were I once with Jesus, fellowship with him will never tire me : ' So shall we be ever with the Lord.' "

In the afternoon he lay down on his bed; and being asked, after he awoke, how he was, he replied, " I am no worse; I am just a monument of mercy, and that is a great deal for such a sinner, especially when I add, that I am hoping for ' redemption through Christ's blood, even the forgiveness of my sins, according to the riches of his grace.' "

" If doubting, disputing, and trampling on his kindness, could have made him change his love, it had never been continued towards me. Though I have not been left to commit gross crimes, yet he and I know the outrageous wickedness of my heart; such wickedness as would have provoked any but a God of infinite love to have cast me into hell; yet, lo! instead of casting me there, he taketh me into his bosom and says to me, ' I have loved thee with an everlasting love, and with loving-kindness have I drawn thee.' ' I will heal their backslidings; I will love them freely.' "

" Oh ! how the Lord hath borne and carried me! He hath, indeed, given me my stripes, but never except when I richly deserved them. ' Oh, that men would praise the Lord for his goodness, and for his wonderful works to the children of men ! ' "

" I was young when left by my parents, yet their instructions, accompanied with God's dealings, made such impressions on my heart as I hope will continue with me to all eternity. I have served many masters, but none so kind as Christ; I have dealt with many honest men, but no creditor like Christ; and had I ten thousand bodies, they should all be employed in labouring for his honour."

Seeing two or three persons of his acquaintance sitting round him, he said, " Now, sirs, I have sinned longer, and in more aggravated forms, than any of you; but what sins cannot the blood of Christ wash out! What cannot mercy forgive! 'The Lord passed by, and proclaimed his name, The Lord, the Lord God, merciful and gracious, long-suffering, and abundant in goodness and truth.' Oh! how astonishing that the Spirit of God should' enter into our vile hearts, contrary to our strivings! Even so it seemeth good in his sight! Let praise flow, for ever flow!"

March 22.—He had no sooner sat down to breakfast, than, like a man enraptured with the views of glory, he gave vent to his feelings by repeating the following lines :—

> " ' They with the fatness of thy house
> Shall be well satisfy'd;
> From rivers of thy pleasures thou
> Wilt drink to them provide.' "
>
> PSALM xxxvi. 8.—*Scotch Version.*

These lines he repeated thrice, changing the words *they* and *them* into *we* and *us;* after which he added, " Oh! how strange that 'rivers of pleasure' should be provided for the murderers of God's Son, and the contemners of his Word!"

One of his sons alleging to him that he seemed to be quite indifferent about things here, he replied,

" Indeed, I am so ; only I would wish you my sons, my friends, my congregation, the Church, and all the world, so far as is consistent with the decree of God, were with Christ. From all other things my mind is weaned; yet, if the influence of God's Spirit were to be withdrawn for a moment, oh how horridly my heart would blaspheme ! "

To one of his hearers, whose father was an eminent Christian, he gave the following advice : " Well, mind these words, ' Thou art my God, I will prepare thee an habitation; my father's God, I will exalt thee.' We should reckon him a madman who would throw away a father's estate, but he is much more foolish who throws away a father's God."

Being told that the day was cold, and that therefore his taking a drive would perhaps hurt him, he said, " Oh, to win to the everlasting day of fellowship with Christ ! Then we shall reflect with pleasure on all our cold and sorrowful days here."

" For a poor man, a dying man, a man that hath much to do, there is no friend like Christ."

Washing his face in water, he said, " Oh, to be washed in the water of life ! " One remarking that he looked better than he did, " It may be so," he replied; " however, when I am conformed to the image of Christ, I shall look far better still." These last words he uttered with a pleasant smile.

Stepping into the chaise to take his ride, and finding himself unable to do it without assistance, he desired his friends to look and see the propriety of that advice,—" Let not the wise man glory in his

wisdom, neither let the mighty man glory in his
might, let not the rich man glory in his riches : but
let him that glorieth glory in this, that he under-
standeth and knoweth me, that I am the Lord which
exercise loving-kindness, judgment, and righteousness, in the earth."

Being asked, on his return from his ride, how he
was, he answered, " Well, well for such a sinner."

To another, who inquired if he felt himself any
easier, he replied, " I cannot say that I am, but I
am just as well as my heart could wish, if I were but
free of sin."

When a third acquaintance asked a similar question, he answered, " I am well; for it is with both
body and soul as it pleaseth God ; and what pleaseth
him as a new-covenant God, I desire to say pleaseth
me too." A saying of Dr Evans, showing his resignation to the rod, being read to him, he said, " Well,
that is just what I would have been at too. Oh !
what kindness has God heaped upon me since the
year —— ! What kind strugglings ! What kind
smilings ! What kind overlookings of my outrageous
wickedness ! He hath shown himself to be God,
and not man, in his dealings with me."

" In my mad attempts he hath often stopped me ;
my mad wishes he hath refused to grant ; and my
mad words he hath often seemed to overlook."

Being asked if he remembered preaching on that
text, Ps. lxxiii. 22, " So foolish was I, and ignorant;
I was as a beast before thee ; " he replied, " Yes, I
remember it very well ; and I remember, too, that

when I described the beast, I drew the picture from my own heart. But, oh! amazing consideration, 'Nevertheless, I am continually with thee: thou hast holden me by my right hand!'"

In the evening, when a friend proposed that his clothes should be taken off, he said, "Very well; I would not wish to be a man of strife on the borders of eternity, and especially when I am as sure that the redeeming God is mine own, as that there is an eternity."

March 23.—One speaking to him about a sermon which he once preached on these words, Isa. xlvi. 4, "Even to your old age I am he," he observed, that he remembered discoursing on that text; and then added, "I must say, that I never yet found God to break his word in this; no, notwithstanding all the provocations which I have given him."

Walking in the grass park which was contiguous to his house, and finding he was scarcely able to move forward, by reason of a boisterous wind, he said to a relation who attended him, "I find I am but weak,—but,

> 'Soon may the storms of trouble beat
> The house of bondage down,
> And let the prisoner fly.'"

WATTS.

When he had taken his rest in the afternoon, he awoke uttering these words, "Oh! what a wonder that I have not slept into eternal life!—rather, oh! what a wonder if I should thus sweetly sleep into eternal life! Oh! what is this!"

Having sat down to tea, he appeared to be in a peculiarly holy frame of mind, and could not forbear making mention of the loving-kindness of the Lord. " Oh ! " he cried, " ' God is love ; ' there is no enmity in him at all ! " Again, " There are three things which are very sweet,—the sovereignty, the free-ness, and the fulness of divine grace." Shortly after, he broke out in the following expressions : " Oh ! wonderful, wonderful subject, *Grace !* Oh ! wonder-ful, wonderful means, by which it vents, *The righ-teousness of Christ !* and wonderful, wonderful issue, *Eternal life !* "

An acquaintance asking him if he really wished to be strong, he replied, " I rather wonder that I have so much health and strength as I have. Many of my fellow-sinners, and many less sinners than I, are now roaring in the place of torment, without any hopes of deliverance, while my body is easy, and my heart is in some measure filled with his praise. The strength which I now wish, is strength ' to walk up and down in the name of the Lord.' "

March 24.—At breakfast, seeing his friends sit-ting around, he said, " Oh, sirs ! when shall I take the last Christian meal with you ? I am not weary of your company, nor have I any cause ; but I would fain be at that, ' I will go to God's altar, even unto God my exceeding joy.' "

One of his little children coming to inquire for his welfare, he desired her to come near ; and putting his hand upon her head, he spoke to her in the fol-lowing manner : " Now, my little dear, oh mind to pray unto God: your father must soon leave you; but cry unto Jesus, ' Thou art my Father, and the guide of my youth;' and then, though you will not have a room like this to come and see your father in, you will be taken to a far better Father's room." This little girl died about three years after.

Being told that his eldest son was gone home, he took occasion to remark how happy he would be if the time of his departure into the eternal world were come. "Oh!" said he, "that I were ready for going home too. About the year ——, these words were sweet to my soul,—' There remaineth a rest for the people of God.'" "Are you not willing, sir," said one, "to live and preach Christ?" He answered, "I would love to preach Christ, if I live; but as to my life, I have no will in that matter. I wish to have my inclinations subordinate to the will of God."

A friend observing that the gospel was said to be spreading in the Established Church of England,— "Oh!" said he, "well, well may it spread. The gospel is the source of my comfort, and every sinner is as welcome to this source as I. And, oh how pleasant, that neither great sins nor great troubles do alter these consolations! These words were once sweetly impressed upon my heart, ' Where sin abounded, grace did much more abound.' Oh! how it delighted me to see God taking advantage of my great sinfulness, to show his great grace!"

"Oh! the sovereignty of God! I think that he hath used more means to bring down the enmity and rebellion of my heart, than he hath used for a hundred beside."

Receiving a glass of wine, he said, " How astonishing that God's Son should get gall and vinegar to drink when his thirst was great, and yet that I should have such wine, when my thirst is by no means excessive!" Afterwards, on a similar occasion, he expressed himself to this effect: "I long to drink of the new wine in my Father's kingdom, which will neither hurt head nor heart. Oh! that I had all the world around me, that I might tell them of Christ!"

A friend reminding him that, through his instrumentality as a teacher of divinity, about sixty or seventy ministers were engaged in preaching Christ, he said, "Had I ten thousand tongues, and ten thousand hearts, and were I employing them all in commendation of Christ, I could not do for his honour as he hath deserved, considering his kindness to such a sinner."

When at tea, he gave vent to his grateful heart in the following words: "I am much obliged to you all, and particularly to you," (addressing himself to his wife,) "for your kindness to me; yet I must go back to this, 'Whom have I in heaven but thee? and there is none upon earth that I desire besides thee.'"

"'He hateth putting away,'—I am sure I have found that; for, oh! the provocations which I have given to God to cast me off; and yet to this day he crowneth me with loving-kindnesses! How astonishing the necessity of the love of the Son of God! Once I thought that I got a ravishing sight of the

necessity of his loving me, *the sinner.*   He said,
' Other sheep I have; them also I *must* bring.'"

" Oh! his kindness, his kindness!   I have shared
of his frowns, as well as of his smiles,—little frowns
in comparison of what I deserved!   Yet, even when I
abused these frowns, as well as his smiles, he hath
often overcome me with tender mercies."

To some who asked him if he was any worse, he
answered, " I am weak, but I am well, considering
that I am such a sinner.   I may say, ' Goodness and
mercy have followed me all the days of my life;'
and I hope to ' dwell in the house of the Lord for
ever.'"

On his supper being spoken of, he said, " Oh! to
be there, where they ' hunger no more, neither thirst
any more; but are filled with the fatness of God's
house!'"

One of his younger children he exhorted in this
manner: "Now, cry to God, ' Thou art my Father.'
I do not think that I was much older than you when
God caused me to claim him; and, oh! God hath
been good to me!   It is long since he said, 'Leave
thy fatherless children; I will preserve them alive,
and let thy widows trust in me.'   As I know not
but I am dying of this distress, I have essayed to
cast you on the Lord; see that you cast yourself on
him."

March 25.—" Long ago I thought to have known
by experience what is meant by ' dying in the Lord.'
That is a lesson, however, which I have not yet
learned; but I will not quit hopes of learning it still."

"Were it not that the blood of Christ cleanseth from all sin, damnation would be my lot; but 'in him I have redemption through his blood, according to the riches of his grace.' And if Christ be glorified to the highest, and I ashamed to the lowest, I am content."

"These words were once sweet to my soul, 'I am less than the least of his mercies.' I thought that I was not worthy of the smallest favour, yet I aimed to apprehend the greatest gift. Oh! amazing scheme, redemption! Amazing contrivance of it by God the Father! Amazing work of the Son purchasing it! Amazing application of it by the Holy Ghost! And amazing possession of it by men!"

"It is now many years since God put me into the state that I could not totally apostatise from him; though no thanks to me, for I have done my utmost against him, and yet he hath held me. I know not if there ever was a sinner such a perverse wretch as I."

One asking him if he remembered who it was that said on his death-bed, that God had fulfilled all the promises in the 91st Psalm to him but the last, "His eyes shall see my salvation," and now he was going to receive the accomplishment of that too, he said, "No;" and added, raising his voice, "But I know a man to whom almost all the lines of that psalm have been sweet. I think, if ever God touched my heart, he went through that psalm with me."

March 26.—Being asked how he had slept, he answered in his usual style, "Good rest for such a sinner." The friend said, "You know that He giveth his beloved sleep." "It is true," replied he, "but sure God hath no cause to love me."

"Long ago, Jehovah silenced me with this, 'Is there any thing too hard for the Lord?' and to this day I have never found out the thing, though perhaps I have resisted his Spirit more than ever a sinner did."

"I wish to be at that point,—He hath put to me the 'everlasting covenant, ordered in all things and sure; for this is all my salvation and all my desire.'"

On his expressing his resignation in this way, "I am entirely at the Lord's will," an acquaintance remarked to him, that "such resignation was not the attainment of every Christian," he answered, "This is rather what I would be at, than what I have attained."

Happening to speak about the students of divinity who had been under his charge, he said, "I wish them all more serious and diligent than ever I have been. I hope, however, that God will not cast me off as a slothful and wicked servant. I am sure that he 'hateth putting away.'"

A friend observing that "it is an unspeakable mercy that God does not deal with us according to our works," he replied, "Ah! if God were to deal with men that way, (I will not except the Apostle Paul,) the hottest place in hell would be the lot of us ministers."

"I think the early death of my father and mother,

the death of a wife and of children, wrought in a remarkable way for my good. I could not but notice, that when God took away these, he always supplied their room with himself. May he deal thus with you when I die!"

"My mind is now so wavering, that I have little remembrance of what is past, little apprehension of what is present, and little foresight of what is future. But, oh! what a mercy, that when once the everlasting arms of Jesus are underneath, he will not lose his hold. 'Israel shall be saved in the Lord with an everlasting salvation.'"

"Here is a wonder,—a sinner saved by the blood of God's Son! There are wonders in heaven, and wonders on the earth; but the least part of redemption work is more wonderful than them all."

March 27.—When some of his relations expressed their wishes for his recovery, "I wish," said he, "that God may do what is most for his glory, and for the good of my soul. Were it left to me whether I would choose life or death, I would not turn a straw for either, but would refer it wholly to God himself. All my days I have been rebelling against and vexing his Holy Spirit, yet I may say this has been the sum of his conduct toward me, 'He wrought for his name's sake, that it should not be polluted.'"

"Oh! how God hath exemplified that law in his conduct toward me: 'If thine enemy hunger, feed him; if he thirst, give him drink;' and in so doing I hope he hath heaped hot, melting coals of fire upon my head."

One of his brethren in the ministry coming in to see him, he spoke to him to this effect: "Now, I am obliged to you for your kindness; but, oh! entreat Christ to pay me a visit. I do you no wrong when I say, that I would not give half-an-hour's visit of Christ for days, or months, or years of yours."

"Any thing that I know about religion is this, that I have found weakness and wickedness about myself; and grace, mercy, and loveliness about Jesus."

When a friend remarked to him, that we must run deeper and deeper in debt to divine grace, he replied, "Oh yes, and God is a good creditor; he never seeks back the principal sum, and indeed puts up with a poor annual-rent."

A number of his acquaintances sitting round him while he took dinner, he broke out with these words, "Well, sirs, may we all at last meet at the table above, and enjoy a feast there; no pain, no complaining, no trouble there, but there is everlasting peace and joy."

"Oh! how strangely Christ hath stuck to me! Perhaps not one in hell ever gave more opposition. His cords of love which he threw about me, I cast away; the words which he spake to me I contemned; yet I think he hath made me to yield."

"I never deserved another word but this, 'Depart from me, ye cursed, into everlasting fire;' but Christ hath spoken far other words to me; and oh! how enlightening, melting, and healing, their influence hath been!"

"What a mercy that God himself enableth us to

believe! for that unbelief of our hearts would call all the promises rank lies, if God did not stop its mouth."

Asking if this were Saturday, he was told No, it was Tuesday, and that he seemed to long for the Sabbath; " I do weary," replied he, " for the Sabbath; and I would fain be at wearying for the everlasting Sabbath. Then I shall have no need of the assistance of preachers; nor will I even need the blessed Bible itself. God's face will serve me for preachers and Bible too."

March 28.—" Oh! that is a strange text, ' God so loved the world, that he gave his only-begotten Son, that whosoever believeth in him should not perish, but have everlasting life.' This declaration would set our hearts all on fire, if they were not infernally frozen; and indeed, closely applied by the Holy Ghost, it would set them on fire, even though infernally frozen. He once applied it with such power to my soul, that I think the application would have inflamed the heart of a devil, had it been so spoken to him."

To his sons in the ministry he repeated the exhortations which he gave them before: " Oh! labour, labour to win souls to Christ. I will say this for your encouragement, that when the Lord led me out to be most earnest in this way he poured in most comfort into my own heart, so that he gave me my reward in my bosom; and when I have tried to help vacancies, he hath repaid me well with glimpses of his glory. Were the Lord to make me young again,

I think I would study to devise other means for gaining souls than those which I have used, and prosecute them with more activity than ever I did."

To an acquaintance who inquired about his health, he gave this account : " I am but weak, but it is delightful to find one's self weak in the everlasting arms. Oh! how much do I owe my Lord!"

" What a mercy that once within the covenant there is no getting out of it again! Now I find my faculties much impaired." His relations answering that it was only his memory which seemed to be affected, he said, "Well; oh! how marvellous that God hath continued my judgment, considering how much I have abused it; and continued my hope of eternal life, though I have misimproved it! ' But where sin hath reigned unto death, grace hath reigned through righteousness, unto eternal life, by Christ Jesus our Lord.' "

" My memory is much failed, but were death once over, I will remember God's heaping of mercies on me, and my multiplied provocations of him; and when I view the first on one side, and the last on the other, on a new-covenant footing, I will sing thanksgivings to God for ever."

Speaking about sermons he remarked, " So far as ever I observed God's dealings with my soul, the flights of preachers sometimes entertained me; but it was Scripture expressions which penetrated my heart, and that in a way peculiar to themselves."

To one who alleged that if he were not happy hereafter, many had reason to be afraid, he gave a reply to the following effect:—" I have no other ground for expecting to be happy than what is by redemption through the blood of Christ, and that is suited to you as well as me."

Expressing his resignation to the will of God, one of his relations observed, that he seemed to sway to one side and his friends to another,—" I own," said he, " that I do sway to one side ; for ' I desire to depart and to be with Christ, which is far better,' and you selfishly wish me to live with you." The relation answering that he hoped it was not wholly selfishness with them; perhaps it was for the good of the church that they desired his life prolonged, he replied, " Indeed it may be selfishness with us both : I confess it may be selfishness in me to wish to be with Christ; but, oh! that God had never seen any other selfishness in me than that!"

" Oh! what must Christ be in himself, when he sweetens heaven, sweetens Scriptures, sweetens ordinances, sweetens earth, and sweetens even trials! Oh! what must Christ be in himself!"

" Oh! to have all our troubles sanctified to us! and then, when in the eternal world, we will with pleasure look back and see, that ' through fire and water he brought us to the wealthy place.' "

One of his children saying to him, " Father, we would fain have you to live;" he answered, " Well, I believe so; but I would fain be with Christ." " But," said the other, "would you not wish to take us with you ? " He replied, "It is not I but Christ who must do that. However, as to my departure, I will not set the time of it to God; he is wise and I am a fool."

Being told that he had done much good to souls since the year 1764, when he said he wished to be gone, he said, " Oh! how strange that God should make use of one so sinful as I to do good to others! But I believe that he was wiser than me; and I shall see this more clearly when in the eternal state."

Ralph Erskine's poem, entitled " The Work and Contention of Heaven," being read to him, he remarked, " Well, though I should never wish to see contention in the Church on earth, yet I should be willing to join in Ralph's contention above. Were I once in heaven, I think that I would contend with the best of them; and I know that our contentions there will not raise heats, but excite love to one another."

On receiving a glass of wine, he with a smile said to his friends, " Now, sirs, I wish you all new wine in the kingdom of our Father at last,—and new wine from the kingdom of our Father while you are on the way to it."

At supper he, with his usual cheerfulness, repeated these lines :—

> " They with the fatness of thy house
>   Shall be well satisfied," &c. ;

and then added, " If earth transformed, partly by the instrumentality of men, is so delicious, oh! what must the fatness of God's house be, the flesh and blood of the Son of God!"

March 29.—Among the first words which he uttered were these: " Oh! what a rebellious child I have been to God! and oh! what a kind Father he hath been to me! I need not go farther than myself to see that ' God is love,' for even in my trouble, he treats me as a mother doth her only sucking child."

A friend happening to say, " I suppose you make not your labours for the good of the Church the ground of your comfort," he replied with uncommon earnestness, " No, no, no! it is the finished righteousness of Christ which is the only foundation of my hope. I have no more dependence on my labours than on my sins. I rather reckon it a wonder of mercy that God took any of my labours off my hand: ' Righteousness belongeth unto him, but unto me shame and confusion of face.' If the Lord were to render to me according to my works, the hottest place in hell would be my reward; yet by Christ's work, eternal life to the most worthless wretch is but a suitable recompense."

Taking a walk through the house, and the sun shining in his face, as he stepped along, he repeated these lines in the 89th Psalm :—

> " In brightness of thy face, O Lord,
>   They ever on shall go.
>   They in thy name shall all the day
>   Rejoice exceedingly ;
>   And in thy righteousness shall they
>   Exalted be on high."
>
> *Scotch Version.*

" Oh, that will be sweet, when the redeemed of

the Lord shall walk thus in heaven," said he; and
then added, with tears in his eyes, " And I am sure
that I may think shame to appear among them; but
the more shame and disgrace I deserve, the more
glory God will get. Oh, what strange things God
hath done to save me! By afflictions in my own
body, by the deaths of my parents, by bringing me
to ordinances, by reproofs of conscience, he hath
striven with me for my salvation."

Walking out to the grass park behind his house,
and happening to speak about the Antiburgher
meeting-house, which was at a little distance from it,
he could not forbear showing his zeal for the good
of souls. " I would be happy," said he, " if my
Antiburgher brother had ten for my one, as crowns
of joy at the last day, though I must say that I would
wish to have as many as possible ; but, oh! it will
be a strange honour for such a wretch as I to have
half-a-dozen."

March 30.—To one who inquired about his welfare, he said, " I sit here an instance of human frailty,
and, I would fain add, an amazing instance of God's
kindness in redemption."

Some persons speaking about an ill bargain in his
hearing, he took occasion to remark, " Oh! how
happy to have an interest in Christ! That is a
bargain which will never break ; and by that, we,
though naturally heirs of hell, are entitled to eternal life."

Often he said, " I find that I am not strong ; but,
oh! it is a wonder that I am not damned! I bless

God that I know at least this much about religion, —I am convinced that I am as a beast before God."

March 31.—"I remember that, about the year ———, I was breathing out slaughter against the Lord Jesus; but that was always the turn of the tale, 'Yet I obtained mercy.' If I were offered the crown of Britain, instead of the fellowship with Christ which I then enjoyed, I would not hesitate a moment about choosing the latter.

"Oh! the debt of grace is a strange kind of debt! Were I even now two or three hundred pounds in debt to any man, it would considerably distress me; but the views of my debt to free grace remarkably refresh my heart."

April 1.—"Were I once in heaven, a look of Christ will cure my broken memory, and all my other weaknesses. There I shall not need wine nor spirits to recruit me; no, nor shall I mind them, but as Christ was through them kind to me."

Seeing the fire stirred, he said, "Oh, to have my heart stirred, and set in an eternal flame of love to that dear Son of God, of whom I think I can say, 'He loved me, and gave himself for me;' and I am sure, in point of worthlessness, he might as well have loved Beelzebub himself."

April 3.—Sitting down in the park behind his house, and the sun shining bright upon his face, he cried out in a kind of ecstasy, "Oh, how pleasant to be for ever beholding the Sun of Righteousness in heaven! and how pleasant, even in time, to see him by faith!"

I

One of his brethren in the ministry paying him a
visit, and saying, among other things, " Sir, we cannot well want you ; " he replied, " O yes, you can
easily want me, and I would wish to be with Jesus.
Meantime, I am wholly at the Lord's disposal. If the
Lord would make me useful in the Church, I have no
objections against living ; but if not, I would rather
die." Upon his friend remarking that the Lord
seemed to be very kind to him, he said, " Yes, God
hath been heaping favours upon me the sinner these
forty years past; and I will say to his honour, that he
hath made my days of affliction always the happiest.
Indeed, I think that I have seldom had very sweet
days, except when I have met with affliction one way
or another." Being asked by his brother if he felt
no uneasiness at leaving his family and congregation,
he answered, " I cannot say that I feel any such uneasiness ; not but that I regard them, but I know that
a God in Christ can infinitely more than supply my
room. I might be spared, and be of little use to
them ; but God will be infinitely useful. My parents
were taken from me when I was young, and God
has been far better to me since than they could have
been." " What think you," said the friend, " of the
present state of the Church ? " He replied, " The
Church is at present in a very poor condition ; but the
Lord can revive her. I have often found, that when
wicked lusts and wicked devils have caused great
disorder in my heart, the Lord hath brought order
out of confusion. This partly encourages me to believe, that though wicked men and wicked devils

cause disorder in the Church, yet the Lord will make all things to work together for good to his own elect. I do not expect to see it; yet it is the joy of my heart, that the time is coming when 'the kingdoms of this world shall become the kingdoms of our Lord and of his Christ.' Dead Churches shall yet be quickened, apostate Churches shall yet be recovered, and Churches shall be planted where there were none before."

April 4.—Finding himself very feeble, he said, " My legs are of little use, my head is of little use, and my hands are of little use ; but my God in Christ is the same to me now as ever."

Speaking about the Associate Synod, which was to meet in the month of May, he said, that he believed he would not be able to attend it; and then added, "Oh, if the Spirit of God would bring me to the General Synod of the Church of the first-born, that would be far better ! No idle words, no angry speeches, no sinful ignorance, no haughty pride there. After all, it is a mercy that Jesus, the great manager of the Church, can over-rule even our contentions here for his own glory."

April 5.—When he took his walk in the park, he pointed to several spots where he said his soul had been ravished with the views of divine grace. " Yea," said he, " on certain occasions my soul hath been so transported there, that, as the apostle speaks, ' whether I was in the body, or out of the body, I could scarcely tell.' Perhaps it is superstitious in me, but I confess I have a peculiar love for these very spots."

Finding, after he came in to the house, himself

tired with his walk, he expressed the feelings of his mind in these words: "Oh! that will be a pleasant journey, ' The ransomed of the Lord shall return, and come to Zion with songs and everlasting joy upon their heads; they shall obtain joy and gladness, and sorrow and sighing shall flee away.'"

Talking about mercy, he remarked, "I could wish to live and die a deep, deep debtor to mercy, and that none of my works should ever be mentioned but as manifestations of mercy, in enabling such a sinner to do any thing for the honour of the God of mercy, and for promoting the work of mercy in the welfare of others."

To an acquaintance, who came to ask for his welfare, he said, "Well, you see I am a prisoner here in my own house; but, oh! that is a happy (I do not choose to call it imprisonment), a happy sort of confinement, in a Redeemer's arms, and in the covenant of grace."

April 6.—" How true is that saying, 'Man in his best estate is altogether vanity!' I am not one of the oldest, yet I find myself exceedingly feeble. However, although I am weak, I have reason to be thankful I am not damned.

" Oh! the sovereignty of God, in permitting some, both angels and men, to fall into misery, while it secures the happiness of the rest to all eternity!"

As an evidence of the tenderness of his conscience, it may be mentioned that he frequently gave this hint to his wife, " I hope you will take care, when I am speaking to any acquaintance, that I do not say

any thing trifling to them. It is not my honour that
I mind in this; but I should be vexed, now that I
am a dying man, if I should say any thing to the dishonour of Christ, to the grief of the godly, or to be
a stumbling-block to the wicked. Indeed it would
be ill on my part to act thus."

Being in conversation with a brother in the ministry, Dunfermline was mentioned. Upon this he
said, " That in his rovings he was often about that
place, and he recollected the time when he went
over the hills of Cleish, from Gairney Bridge, to hear
that great man of God, Mr Ralph Erskine, whose
ministry, he thought, was brought home by the Spirit
of God to his heart." Being desired to return thanks
after partaking of a meal, he expressed himself in the
following manner: "We thank thee, O Lord, that
since we rove in our weakness, we rove about those
places where we think we met with the God of Bethel,
and saw him face to face."

April 9.—Being asked how he was now, he replied,
" I am weak; but the motto of each of my days is,
' He hath not dealt with us as we have sinned, neither
rewarded us according to our iniquities.'"

Sitting down in the park, and finding his eyes unable to bear the bright shining of the sun, he said,
" Oh! how pleasant to be in that place where they
are so overcome with the glory of the Sun of Righteousness, that they have to cover their faces with their
wings!"

Having occasion to converse about young men
coming out to the ministry, he said, " Well, though

pride prevails much in my heart, yet I think I would trample it thus far under my feet, as that I would be glad to see all my students,—and not they only, but all the faithful ministers of Jesus,—bringing hundreds or thousands of souls with them to heaven, though I should have but five or six."

Taking him into his meeting-house, he looked round him, and said, "Now, weak as I am, I would try to preach yet, if I had none to preach in my stead. Oh! what sweet fellowship with Christ I have had here! That pulpit hath been to me the best place in all the house."

A young surgeon paying him a visit, he took occasion to offer some advices to him. Among other things he remarked, that persons of his profession had excellent opportunities of conversing with dying sinners about their eternal interests; that their patients would probably pay more attention to religious hints from them than from other persons; that while they gave cures to others, they should never forget to apply to Christ for spiritual healing themselves. As he was evidently turning hoarse with speaking, one of his relations reminded him that he was exhausting himself, and begged him to forbear for a little. He replied, "Well, I shall say no more now; but, oh! to be at that,—

> ' My mouth the praises of the Lord
>   To publish cease shall never;
>   Let all flesh bless his holy name
>   For ever and for ever.' "

Ps. cxlv. 21.—Scotch Version.

May 6.—Lying on his back in the bed, and being exceedingly faint, he said in a low tone of voice, " Here is a lecture on that text, ' Vanity of vanities, all that cometh is vanity and vexation of spirit;' for what a poor useless creature am I now! But oh! what a mercy that Christ can raise glory to himself out of mere vanity!" In uttering these last words, his heart seemed to be quite overcome.

When a friend alleged to him that he appeared to be sunk in his spirits, he replied, "I am so; but it is not in the least through any terror, but just through weakness."

Being asked if he was not afraid to enter into a world of spirits, he answered, " No; a persuasion that Christ is mine makes me think, that when I appear in that world, as a new incomer, all the spirits there will use me well on Christ's account."

It being remarked by an acquaintance, that, considering him as a dying man, he seemed to be as easy as he well could be: " Yes," said he, " I really am so; for in my body I am not much pained; and as to my mind, it is composed, or rather cheerful. I mean not that I have what the world calls mirth; but I possess a sort of cheerfulness which ariseth from views of certain texts of Scripture."

May 7.—" As I have had fulness all my days, I believe that I could not now easily bear with pinching want; yet I think, to publish the gospel of Jesus, I could willingly meet with want or any thing else."

Taking his ride in the chaise, and observing how

pleasantly the corn and the grass were growing, he said, " Oh ! I think I should love to see that promise accomplished, ' The wilderness and the solitary place shall be glad for them ; and the desert shall rejoice and blossom as the rose ; it shall blossom abundantly, and rejoice even with joy and singing. The glory of Lebanon shall be given unto it ; the excellency of Carmel and Sharon ; they shall see the glory of the Lord, and the excellency of our God.' Oh ! I should love to see all this ere I die, though I would wish that it may not be long till the event take place. I should love, when I depart to heaven, to be able to tell this news to the redeemed millions, that the Holy Ghost had been remarkably poured out in East Lothian, and that there was now not a family in which the worship of God was not observed. I daresay it delights the redeemed above, to hear of Christ's glory being displayed, and of souls being saved, on earth."

When he observed the concern which his wife showed about his welfare, he said, " Now, no doubt, you do not wish to hear about my departure ; but ' Thy Maker is thy husband ; the Lord of hosts is his name.' He can infinitely more than supply the want of me."

May 8.—Passing by the door of his study, and looking into it, one remarked, " Sir, you never go in there now ;" he answered, " No ; the closet I wish now is the place of God's immediate presence. There the face of God will serve me instead of all my books."

Addressing himself to one of his sons, he said, " Now I am easy whether ever you or any of my

family be what the world calls rich; but I should wish
you all to be the fearers of God. Next to seeing
Christ as he is, I think that I would desire to see
you, and hundreds at your back, all debtors to free
grace. Oh! I would be happy to say, ' Lord, here
am I, and the children which thou hast given me.'

" Ever since God dealt convincingly with my heart,
I never had any comfort in the thought that my sins
were little, but in the belief that the virtue of Christ's
blood is infinite,—blood that ' cleanseth from all sin;'
and in the consideration of God's mercy being higher
than the heavens.

" I once thought that text, ' I will have mercy on
whom I will have mercy,' had just been made for me;
and that it was so full of grace, just that it might
suit my condition. Were it possible for his majesty
and I to become young again, and were it left to my
choice whether I would have his lot or my own, I
would, without hesitation, choose my own. If I have
not got such grand entertainment for the body as he,
I have got feasts on texts of Scripture, the like of
which perhaps he never obtained: ' Goodness and
mercy have followed me.' "

Talking about death, he said, " It might be written on my coffin, ' Here lies one of the cares of Providence, who early wanted both father and mother,
and yet never missed them.' "

May 9.—Speaking of submission to the rod of God,
he said, " I would not wish that foolish question ever
put to me, ' Would you go to hell, if that were the
Lord's will?' for it is God's promise, securing my sal-

vation, that has much influence in making me resigned. God said to me, ' I am the Lord thy God;' and if he were not to be mine for ever, he would forfeit his word,—which is impossible."

Being advised by a friend to give an assignation of his right to his books, for the good of his family, he replied, " No, no; I would not wish that ever there should be the least appearance of avarice of the world in me. I can trust my family to Providence; and if, when I am in heaven, it appear that there was one converted by means of any thing I ever wrote, I will mark down an hundred pounds; if there should be two, I will say, there are two hundred pounds; and if twenty, there is something of more value than two thousand pounds. That is the reward which I wish."

Two young ladies coming in to see him, he asked how they were; and on their answering, " Very well," he said, " ' It is of the Lord's mercies that we are not consumed;' and, oh! never say to your own consciences you are very well, until you have good evidence of your interest in Christ. Be earnest to have acquaintance with Jesus; no connection so glorious as union with Christ; no pleasure like that which is enjoyed in fellowship with him."

To one who observed, that some who saw him thought he was rather better, he replied, " All my wish is, that if God spare me, I may have gifts to serve him while I live; and if I die, I wish to praise him while I have any being."

May 10.—Hearing some talk about endorsing a bill, he said, " Oh how pleasant! The bills of God's promises are my heritage. I have often forgotten them; but I am sure Jehovah minds them; and I know, too, that the Spirit of God will never deceive me."

Speaking about his weakness, he said, " God deals so tenderly with me in my affliction, that indeed I think the strokes, as it were, go nearer his heart than they do mine."

May 11.—" The command is, 'Owe no man anything.' What a mercy there is no such precept as this, 'Owe the Saviour nothing!' or even this, 'Study to owe him as little as possible!'

" I confess I would not like to stand at our town cross, with a paper on my breast, declaring that I was a bankrupt to men; but, oh! I think I should love to stand in the most public place of heaven, having all the redeemed pointing to me as the greatest sinner that ever was saved; yea, I think their very staring at me, as the chief debtor to free grace, would rejoice my heart."

May 14.—When one remarked to him that his memory seemed to be much failed, he replied, " It is so;" and then shutting his eyes, he, in a devout manner, uttered this prayer: " Lord, I am a stranger on this earth; hide not thy commandments from me." Some alleging that he would not get out in the chariot, on account of the wetness of the day, " Well," said he, " if God would send his new-covenant chariot, death, and transport me to heaven ere night, I should be happy, let the day be what it will.

" Oh! what a mercy that my admission into eternal life does not in the least depend on my ability for any thing; but I, as a poor sinner, will win in leaning on Christ as the Lord my righteousness,— on Christ, 'made of God unto me righteousness, sanctification, and redemption!' I have nothing to sink my spirits but my sins; and these need not sink me either, since the Great God is my Saviour."

To one who inquired for his welfare, he said, " I am sitting here, trying to wait for the salvation of God. I should love that my departure were nearer than perhaps you would wish; but I will not murmur."

Taking a walk from one room to another, he, in a sort of transport, cried, " Oh! it will be pleasant to enter into Christ's light room above! Surely when I am there, and when I reflect on the opportunities which I enjoyed in this world, I shall wonder at myself as a fool for the misimprovement of them. But what shall I say? When Christ is the way to heaven, 'a wayfaring man, though a fool, cannot err therein.'"

Advising a young man to honour his father and mother, and being told by a friend that they were dead, he took occasion to remark, " Oh! what a mercy that you can never tell me that my friend Jesus is dead, when so many of my earthly acquaintances are gone! If you say of him that he was dead, I can answer, But now he 'is alive, and lives for evermore; and hath the keys of hell and of death.'"

June 4.—Conversing about the manner in which the gospel call is addressed to men, he remarked,

"It has been my comfort these twenty years, that not only *sensible* sinners, but the most stupid, are made welcome to believe in Christ."

When he lay down on his bed, one asked him how he was now; he answered, "I lie here in the everlasting arms of a gracious God." "Are you not afraid," said the friend, "to appear at the tribunal of God?" He replied, "Were I looking to give the account in my own person, considering my sins, I might indeed be terrified; but then I view Christ the Judge as my Advocate and my Accountant, and I know that I do not owe more debt than he has paid."

June 5.—An acquaintance going to leave him, and saying that he would probably soon see some of his brethren in the ministry, "Tell them," said he, "that it is my desire that they may labour to win souls to Christ, for now I am not able, though ever so willing. Meantime you must say, that Christ hath been a kind Master to me. Many a visit hath he given me already; and I expect to be with him in heaven by-and-by. Tell them, too, that I desire their prayers, that, with submission to the divine will, I may 'depart to be with Christ, which is far better.'"

Being urged to take his breakfast, "I will eat," said he, "as much as I am able. The food is very good in itself, and it is a memorial of my spiritual provision, and I love it not the worse on that account."

When he coughed sore, and a relation expressed his grief to see him in such distress, "Why not cough?" replied he; "oh! it would be happy, if each of these coughs and throwings would hasten me to God as 'my exceeding joy.'"

One remarking to him that his tongue seemed to be very foul, he answered, "It may be so, but what a mercy that it is not tormented in flames! Oh! the power of free grace, that can make a tongue, which is a world of iniquity, an everlasting praiser of Christ in heaven! But what need I say, for 'the heart is deceitful above all things, and desperately wicked,' and yet it is made an eternal habitation of God and the Lamb!"

When he came in from his ride, he had scarcely sat down, when he began expressing his admiration of the love of God: "Oh! the sovereignty of grace! How strange, that I, a poor cottager's son, should have a chaise to ride in! and what is far more wonderful, I think God hath often given me rides in the chariot of the new covenant! In the former case he hath raised me from the dunghill, and set me with great men; but in the latter he hath exalted the man, —sinful as a devil,—and made him to sit with the Prince of the kings of the earth. Oh, astonishing! astonishing! astonishing!"

Being offered a little wine, he objected to taking it. "I am afraid," said he, "that it will hurt me; and I would not wish to hurt that head, which, as well as my heart, is Christ's. Let him do with it as he pleaseth, but I would not wish to have any hand in hurting it myself."

"No doubt I would love to be at my public work

again; and had it been any other than God that had restrained me, I would not have taken it well; but as it is the Lord, I desire to submit."

"Were God to present me with the dukedom of Argyle on the one hand, and the being a minister of the gospel, with the stipend which I have had, on the other, so pleasant hath the ministry been to me, notwithstanding all my weakness and fears of little success, I would instantly prefer the latter."

To some acquaintances who came to visit him, he said, "Here, sirs, take warning that ye must die. Now I think it is come to dying work with me; but, if Jesus hold me up, though I die all is well. 'Blessed are the dead who die in the Lord.'"

A minister asking him what was the best method one could take when a consideration of his own sinfulness terrified him in preaching? he made this reply, "Attempt to believe,—just as a *sinner*,—as the *chief of sinners*. Those promises have been sweetest to me which extend to men, if they are but out of hell. 'It is a faithful saying, and worthy of all acceptation, that Christ Jesus came into the world to save sinners, of whom I am chief.' Once these words were sweet to my soul. I thought, ill as I was, I could not be worse than the chief of sinners. Conscience said that I was the most wicked wretch that ever breathed, and that I had showed myself to be such, especially by rebelling against convictions, and by trampling on Christ's alluring words; yet, since Christ came to save sinners, even the chief, why, thought I, should I except myself?"

When he rose to take a walk through the house, he found himself so feeble, that he was in danger of falling at almost every step. However, he comforted himself and his friends in this manner, "I am now very weak; but were I in heaven I shall 'renew my strength.' There I 'shall mount up with wings as an eagle; I shall run, and not be weary; I shall walk, and not faint.' No staggerings there."

After family worship in the evening, he remarked, "Oh! it would be pleasant if our experiences in ordinances were such here, as that they would fit us for the exercises of heaven; our prayers here, a stretching forth of our desires for the enjoyment of God, and of the Lamb; and our praises here, a tuning of our hearts for the songs above."

June 6.—One asking him this question, "Sir, does it not strike you with fear, when you think of being confined in a grave?" he answered, "No; such is my esteem of Christ, that I think I am easy though they should bury me in a dunghill, if my soul were but with him." "But," said the other, "are you not sorry to part with all your family?" He replied, "I must own that I have a concern about my wife and children; but when my heart enters properly into these words, 'Be with the Lord,'—the leaving of them diminishes into a very small point: and although natural affection for them is as strong as ever, I hope that, when I am away, Christ will far more than supply my room to them; and then, you see, we shall be better on all hands."

Seeing his relatives assisting him under his weakness, he often said, " I really wonder at the kindness of men to me; but especially I am amazed, when I reflect that it is all the kindness of my God, through them."

When on any occasion his little children were gathered around him, he used to commend Christ Jesus in such words as these: " There is none so glorious as Christ; ' he is altogether lovely.' If you could put all the gold and silver into one heap, the glory of Christ would far exceed all. I say this, having, I think, seen Jesus: but as yet I have seen him only ' through a glass darkly;' after this I hope to see him ' face to face.'"

To one of his sons in the ministry he gave the following advice: " Oh! try to run as deep in Christ's debt as possible; and take his own way of paying, viz., by acknowledging his kindness. And when you mind your own debt, remember your father's debt too: say, ' Thou art my God, I will praise thee; my father's God, I will exalt thee.'" Again, " Oh! labour, labour to win souls to Christ; souls are well worth the winning, and Christ is far more worthy of winning them to. It gives me pleasure now to think that I did not indulge myself in idleness in my Master's service; not but that I was idle, only I do not remember indulging myself in it."

June 15.—A friend saying to him, " You are not now travelling to Stow sacrament, as you used to do about this time of the year," he replied to this purpose, " No, I wish to be travelling to God, as ' my exceeding joy.' In the meantime I must say, that at Stow

K

I have had such sweet hours, that neither Christ nor I shall ever forget them."

Being asked what he thought of free grace, after being so many years a minister? "I," said he, "have altered my mind about many things, but I am now of the same mind that ever I was as to grace and salvation through Christ."

"Where are now all your anxieties about the Church?" said one. "I have left," he replied, "my anxiety about it, and about every thing else, on the Lord: and, indeed, were it not for a God in my nature, I would reckon the present case of the Church very hopeless; but in the view of Christ, I am persuaded that she will yet remarkably revive on earth."

June 17.—He had now become extremely weak; but, "as the outward man decayed the inward man was renewed day by day."

Lying on his bed, and scarcely able to speak, he looked up to one of his brethren in the ministry, and said, with a smile, "Oh! Mr ——, 'the Lord is my strength and my song; and he also is become my salvation.'"

June 18.—Seeing him much distressed under the failing of nature, a friend said to him, "Sir, I hope the Lord is not forsaking you now." "No," he answered; "God is an unchanging Rock."

Being asked by another how he was, he replied, "Oh! it is strange that the Lord Jesus encourageth us to pray even at the last!"

Fixing his eye on two or three of his relations at his bedside, he addressed them in the most affecting manner. "Oh, Sirs! dying-work is serious!—serious work indeed! and that you will soon find, strong as you now are."

June 19.—He seemed to be frequently engaged in speaking; but, owing to the change in his voice, it was only a very few of his words which could be understood.

Upon a friend saying to him, "Sir, you seem to be sore distressed;" it was thought he made this answer, "The Lord hath his own way of carrying on his own work."

The last words which he was heard to utter were these: "MY CHRIST!"

About four hours after, he fell asleep in Jesus. His mortal remains were interred the following Saturday in Haddington churchyard, where a monument to his memory was erected by his relatives, with the following inscription:—

TO

THE MEMORY

OF

MR JOHN BROWN,

THIRTY-SIX YEARS MINISTER OF THE GOSPEL

AT HADDINGTON,

AND TWENTY YEARS PROFESSOR OF DIVINITY

UNDER THE ASSOCIATE SYNOD.

AFTER MAINTAINING AN EMINENT CHARACTER

FOR PIETY, CHARITY, LEARNING, AND DILIGENCE,

HE DIED

REJOICING IN HOPE OF THE GLORY OF GOD,

AND ADMIRING THE RICHES OF DIVINE GRACE TO HIM

AS A SINNER,

THE 19TH OF JUNE, A.D. 1787,

AGED 65 YEARS.

BLESSED ARE THE DEAD WHICH DIE IN THE LORD: THEY REST FROM THEIR LABOURS, AND THEIR WORKS DO FOLLOW THEM."

Mr Brown left behind him a widow, Mrs Violet Croumbie, and four sons and two daughters. She was the daughter of Mr William Croumbie, Stenton, East Lothian, and survived him nearly thirty-five years, having died at Edinburgh, March 18, 1822. The whole of his family by both his marriages have now gone " the way of all the earth," with the exception of him who pens these lines.

SELECT REMAINS.

SELECT REMAINS.

LETTERS.

Sir,—Despise not the day of small things,—I might say, of good things. When you consider yourself as one of the first-rate deservers of damnation, how may you admire the great kindness of God! Compare your mercies, your visits, not with the wishes of your soul, but with the desert of your sin; and then 'a little one will appear as a thousand, and a small one as a strong nation' of astonishing favours. Though we should get but one smile of his countenance, and hear but one word from his blessed lips, in a whole year,—what a mercy to those who deserve all the year throughout to be tormented in the lowest hell! Bless God for any transient blinks you enjoy; but let the unchangeable Saviour be the only confidence of your soul. Frames, as well as heart and flesh, do fail; but He will never fail you nor forsake you.

You ask me concerning marks of fellowship with

our Lord Jesus. Alas! that I should know so little about that happiness. How easy to talk about spiritual things, when we feel not their power; but, without doubt, our communion with Christ is real, if it make us lie in the dust before him, and cause us to loathe and abhor ourselves before him. Isa. vi. 5, "Then said I, Woe is me! for I am a man of unclean lips, and I dwell among a people of unclean lips: for mine eyes have seen the King, the Lord of hosts." Oh! what a kindly, a heart-humbling, a soul-shaming, and paining view of sin, particularly of inward enmity and unbelief, does the smile, the voice of God, produce! We cannot look on a God of redeeming love, without thinking ourselves unclean—outrageous beasts and devils, Ps. lxxiii. 21, 22 ; and Rom. vii. 24. Real communion, too, melts our hearts with love to God, and to his laws, ordinances, and people; and renders us vexed and ashamed that we cannot love him to purpose, 2 Cor. v. 14. But it is one thing to know these matters in our head, and another thing to feel them in our heart. Ah! how many of us, called Christians, are led like beasts by the *head;* and how few, like saints indeed, are led by the *heart!* Oh, to hear his heart-drawing voice! Oh, to see his soul-attracting countenance! Oh, to be fast bound by the cords of his love, so that neither strong lusts within us, nor numerous devils, nor an evil world, may ever be able to loose us! Wishing that the eternal God,— the dying Redeemer,—may be your all and in all, and the all and in all of your seed,—I am yours, &c.

HADDINGTON, *August* 20, 1765.

LETTER II.

DEAR SIR,—Yours I received. Oh that we had learned Christ to any purpose! It were well to have learned but as much of him as to convince us that he is far above our comprehension. There is nothing in creation, but the more acquaintance we have with it, the more spots and blemishes we shall see; but Christ, the more he is seen and known, appears so much the more comely. Created things answer but a few wants, and that for a little time; but Jesus answers all wants at once, and makes up one for ever and ever. It is truly sad that silly trifles should be able to call off our hearts from him! Oh, it is sad that when Christ is infinitely better than all, he should be chiefly slighted by us! And wretched is our ingratitude, that, when Christ has done so much for us, we should be unwilling to do any thing for him! Oh, what a mercy that he deals not with us as we deserve!

As all lawful business is full of Christ and of eternal things, yours is so in a peculiar manner.* Your asking of persons what they desire, as they come in, is an emblem of Christ's saying, "What will ye that I should do unto you? Buy of me gold tried in the fire, that thou mayest be rich." Your arranging of goods on shelves, puts me in mind of Christ's arranging his blessings in the ordinances of the gospel, and in the various promises. Often you let people see

---

* His correspondent was engaged in trade.

things, and they refuse to buy them at all, or at least to take them at your price,—a sad emblem of our conduct toward Christ! Ah! how often do we come to his ordinances, and buy nothing,—view his covenant in a careless manner, and refuse to have any of his special benefits! We reason with Christ; not to have his blessings cheaper—that cannot be—but to have them at a higher rate than that at which he offers them. Is not this madness with a witness? We can give nothing, and yet will bid something, when Christ tells us that he will not take anything as his price. Oh! cursed is our contempt of Jesus, when we tempt him with any of our things! Perhaps you sometimes exchange goods: but no exchange is like that which Christ made. He took our curse, and gives us his blessing; he took our sorrows, and gives us his joys; he takes our old heart, which is little worth, and gives us a new one; he takes away our filthy garments, and clothes us with change of raiment! You get your own share of slack trade on some days; but if you could learn the way of trading quick with Christ,—if bad debtors make you rightly consider what you owe to Christ, and how poorly you pay, you might make the worst part of your business the most profitable.—Yours, &c.

HADDINGTON, 1769.

LETTER III.

DEAR SIR,—I desire to sympathise with you in your affliction. Experience hath made me know how hard it is to part with a pleasant child. God hath in this dispensation showed you, that " vanity of vanities, all that cometh is vanity." There is no certain source of pleasure besides Christ. When we come into life, we are much in the same situation as you were when you got home,—we find created joys on their death-bed. May we put as little trust in them as they deserve! In this stroke, I am sure, God is righteous. Think if your tender little one did not twine about your heart, and draw it off from God. Is it not then just that God abolish the idol? But, methinks, this stroke is not only *just*, but is *good* also, both to you and to your child. What you have met with on this occasion appears to me an evidence, so far as I can see into the secrets of Jehovah, that God has at once taken your child to himself, and, in some measure, taken your child's room in your heart. Now, if, when young ones are in such danger here, God hath taken your daughter to educate her in heaven, —if she is gone to Christ, your best friend above, as I think, from your concern about her, appears manifest,—is she any worse? rather is she not far better? Do you well to be angry that God has dealt so graciously with her? Learn from the death of children to pant for the ever-living God; to consider them, and all created things, as mere loans, which God may recall at pleasure. Esteem nothing but Christ your proper possession; all things beside him give us the slip.

As to the question which you propose, "How may one know that afflictions are sanctified?" I would answer, If they tend to humble us,—if they open our eyes to discern a vanity in creatures,—if they fill us with resentment at our sin,—if, under them, we would rather choose to get rid of corruption than of trouble, —if we would fain acquiesce in God's will even in smiting us, and are grieved for the risings of our hearts against him,—these are a good sign that our troubles are sanctified. But in order to put all out of doubt, even now try to believe, and lay the burden of your whole salvation upon Jesus, as bearing your griefs and carrying your sorrows; and then, I am sure, your troubles will be sanctified. "Fear not, only believe."

As to the note at the service of the table, of which you spoke, it was to this purpose: "When the savages of Louisiana were going to murder Lasale, or his Italian friend, he told them, that such was his regard for them, that he had them all in his heart; and would they murder a man who loved them so well? At the same time applying a small looking-glass to his breast, he desired them to look and see if it was not so. It is said that the poor savages, observing their own image, had their barbarity melted into the most tender compassion and love; they would not for a world have hurt him, or suffered him to be hurt by others. Now, believing communicants, Jesus bids

you look into his heart, and see yourselves there.
' Behold,' saith he, ' you were in my heart from
eternity, when I undertook for you; then my delights were with the sons of men, and I rejoiced in
the habitable part of the earth. Lo! you were in
my heart on Calvary, when it was melted as the wax
with the wrath due to your crimes! Behold how you
are in my heart now that I am in the midst of the
throne, while I appear in the presence of God for you,
and prepare a place for you!' Will you any more
by sin murder a man,—a God-man, that had, that
has, and that ever will have, you in his heart? Melts
not thy soul into tender affection to him? Startles
not thy heart at the thought of imbruing thy hands
in his blood? Do not all thy inward powers cry out,
' Was I, a very Beelzebub,—a prince of devils,—in
Jesus' heart from everlasting, and shall I be there to
everlasting? Were all his thoughts, thoughts of love
concerning me? Was all his heart inflamed with love
to me, and all inflamed with wrath on my account?
What shall I render to him for his kindness? Doth
the eternal God give me full and everlasting room in
his blessed heart? and shall not I give him some,—
give him all the room in that sty, that hidden hell
of mine? Come in, thou blessed of the Lord; why
standest thou without? Fill the house, my heart, with
thy glory. Let my tongue cleave to the roof of my
mouth if I forget thee, O Jesus! and prefer not
thee to my chiefest joy! O Jesus! go up higher and
higher; and ye created enjoyments, come down, and
sit below his footstool.' "—I am yours, &c.

LETTER IV.

DEAR SIR,--I received yours. I would desire to join with you in prayer for your children. May God write on the afflicted little one his new name. I am glad to find that you receive so many of the tender mercies of God in your afflictions. If you or I get a crumb from the Master's table, what a wonder of sovereign mercy is it! It is quite undeserved, nay, contrary to all our desert. Often it is not desired, or, rather, is half forbidden. What else are our careless prayers, and our careless waiting on ordinances, but a courting the denial of mercies! However, endless praise be to our liberal Jesus, who, seeing our need, doth grant unto us his gracious presence! " His going forth is prepared as the morning, and as the rain that waiteth not for man, and tarrieth not for the sons of men." At this solemnity, I thought that some drops of Heaven's dew fell on my soul. The views of that unmatched Jesus, as my *all*, and *in all*, suiting all my sins, and all my troubles, and all that I could desire, and infinitely more than I could ask or think, were delightful to my heart. But, alas! such is my worse than infernal temper, that, when at any time he begins to touch my heart, or to take me into his embrace, I struggle to get from him; and scarcely are a few minutes past, when I am often seven-fold more like a child of hell than before, in respect of carnality, heart-wanderings, and the like!

Oh, that cursed heart of unbelief, that will forsake our own mercy!

Truly, Sir, when I compare the poor commendations which I give to the unmatched Immanuel, with the conduct of my soul, I am apt to say, Oh! what a dreadful compassing of God with lies and deceit is found in me! May the Lord have mercy on an inward blasphemer! Dear friend, pity me, and cry mightily to God in my behalf. It is shocking, if you knew it, to think what difference there is betwixt my sermons and my own inward life. Oh! what astonishing grace and blood that must be, which can save such devils,—I should say, such sinners worse than devils! —Yet, Oh, to be distinguished debtors to free grace! Oh, happy, happy, to be drowned for ever in debt to redeeming love! Oh to be set up here, and at the last day, and for ever, in the most public place, as bankrupts that owed infinitely much to divine kindness, and that could not pay a farthing!—Yours, &c.

Stow, *June* 6, 1769.

LETTER V.

Dear ——,—Having heard some days ago of your illness, I have transmitted to you the following hints:—

1. Let your days of trouble be days of trying your own heart and way before God; and, oh! let your search be in earnest, as you know not how soon death, and your appearance before the tribunal of Christ,

may actually take place. Mind that it is not the having somewhat of a profession, but the having our soul united to Jesus Christ, and our being renewed in the spirit of our minds, that will stand as real religion before God.

2. Think how much better it will be to discern the mistakes relative to your state, or relative to your thoughts, words, and actions, now, when sovereign grace may rectify them, than to have them discovered when it is too late to obtain a happy change.

3. Ponder under what view Christ answers your case. He is "made of God to you wisdom, righteousness, sanctification, and redemption;" and so is answerable to you, as foolish and ignorant, naked and guilty, corrupted and defiled, imprisoned and in bondage. Think, I beseech you, how he suits you in his new-covenant characters, and how great is your need of him in all these views.

4. Ponder carefully, that Christ, and all the fulness of God, is given unto you in the free promises and offers of the gospel, such as Prov. i. 22, 23, ix. 4, 5, xxiii. 26; Isa. xlv. 22–25, xlvi. 12, 13, lv. 1–7, xlii. 6, 7; John vi. 37; 2 Cor. v. 18–21; Acts xiii. 26; Rev. xxii. 17. See that you do not merely look over and think over these scriptures, but try and apply them to your heart.

5. Rather think too ill of your soul's case before God, and of your conduct in life, than too well. If they cannot stand the trial of such texts as these, Matt. v. 3–8; Rom. viii. 2, vii. 14, 15, 24; 2 Cor. v. 17; Gal. iv. 19, vi. 15; 1 Pet. ii. 7; John xxi. 17, all is naught.

6. Consider what pains God hath been at with you. His language in this rod is plainly, "Oh that they were wise, that they understood this!" And see also John v. 6; Matt. xx. 32; Ezek. xxxiii. 11.

Finally, Mind that all the instructions parents and others have given you, all the offers of salvation which have been made to you, and all the strivings of the Spirit with your conscience, will bear witness against you, if you make not the receiving of Christ, and walking in him, your most earnest study.

"Now," my dear friend, "*now* is the accepted time, now is the day of your salvation." Oh, harden not your heart, but flee for refuge to Jesus, as the hope set before you! May the Lord himself persuade you.—Yours, &c.

LETTER VI.

TO A RELATION, ON THE DEATH OF HER FIRST CHILD.

DEAR ——,—God has indeed manifested, in your case, the vanity of all earthly enjoyments, in giving you a child to look about her and die. However, O mind it is the Lord! let him do what seemeth to him good. She was not given, but lent you. Grudge not the recall of the loan. I am sure he did not recall it till he saw it proper and necessary. In plenty of wisdom, as well as justice, he doth afflict. Nay, in plenty of mercy too, Heb. xii. 6–11; Ps. cxix. 71, Beware of stupidity under his hand, or sinful murmuring at his management. Spend some time in

L

solemn surrendering of yourselves and concerns to God; this is an excellent mean of balancing the affections, and calming the tumultuous passions. I beseech you, beware of immoderate sorrow for the loss of your only child. If you do not, it may break your own delicate constitution, and quickly hurry you to the grave. You have not reason to sorrow as those who have no hope. Why grudge a child to God himself? Cannot he bear, care for, and satisfy her longing soul, better than you? Cannot he be to her better than ten mothers, and better to you than ten daughters? Indulge not your mind in recollecting her agreeable looks and the like, but turn aside, looking unto Jesus, the Child, the Son of God. The Lord demands you to balance matters with him, in thinking on, esteeming, delighting in, and fillin your heart with his infinitely precious Son, instead of your child. Fellowship, close fellowship with him, can allay the bitterest griefs, and make up the greatest losses on earth. Wonder at his mercy, that your husband, as well as your child, is not taken from you. It is of the Lord's mercies that we are not consumed. Oh, to live on his never-dying self, as our all and all!—Yours affectionately, &c.

LETTER VII.*

DEAR ——,—When I get an opportunity, I have

* This and the three following letters were written during his last illness to his two eldest sons, the Rev. John and Ebenezer Brown.

some thoughts of making a trial of the medicine which you mention, though my hopes of being better by it are not very high. My life and health seem now to pass like a declining shadow; nor dare I repine at the matter. God hath, in some measure, satisfied me with old age : I would therefore be longing to see his salvation. I observe several things relative to my family, which urge my carnal heart to wish continuance ; but my death can make no vacancy in my family, and far less in the Church, which Jesus cannot easily fill up. What I desire is, to have the presence of God in my trouble, and to be enabled to act for his glory. I can hardly bear the thought of being consigned to be a useless weight on his earth. But I must not quarrel at his disposal; he cannot but do right ; nor would I wish to attempt making "straight what he has made crooked." " Redemption through his blood, even the forgiveness of sins, according to the riches of his grace," is what I ever desire to enjoy; and I wish to leave the circumstances of my departure to his high sovereign will. If " grace reign through Jesus' righteousness to eternal life" to me and mine, I ask no more. I believe I shall never be perfectly well till I be with " the Lamb in the midst of the throne." In the meantime, I earnestly desire to die as a wax-taper, sending forth a sweet smell of Him whose " garments smell of myrrh, and aloes, and cassia."—I am yours, &c.

LETTER VIII.

DEAR ——,—I am at present in a weak and languishing condition; but as it is the doing of the Lord
I desire to be resigned, and would gladly be content,
whether death or recovery be the issue. Indeed the
desire of my heart is, that, if it be his will, I should
" depart and be with Christ, which is far better" than
being in this sinful world. But it would be improper
for me to set up my ignorant and corrupt will as a
rule to the Most High. I wish to be at entire and
cordial resignation to his will, who hath so graciously
" performed all things for me." Let him recover or
let him kill me, as is most for his glory; I hope that it
will be in infinite love to my soul. I desire to take
all kindly from his hand; and I hope that he will
sweeten all with believing views of his everlasting
love to me. To leave a multitude of kind relations,
hearers, and neighbours, on earth, is an easy matter,
in order to depart, and to be with Jesus Christ for
ever. When I write perhaps my last letter to you, O
that I could commend Him who is " white and ruddy,
the chiefest among ten thousand, and altogether
lovely!" Rather, O that the Holy Ghost would enable
you and your children to come and see him! I am
sure that is a pleasant and enriching sight. May
never one of you get rest in your minds, till you obtain such a blessed discovery! I give it, perhaps as
my last words to you and your children, that there is
none like Christ, there is none like Christ, there is
none like Christ!—Yours affectionately, &c.

LETTER IX.

DEAR ——,—My weakness still continues; nor indeed is my mind anxious about this, but a Christ-glorifying death, and a being for ever with the Lord. My concern, too, is that all my relations should have my place on earth delightfully supplied, by the knowledge, care, and fellowship of Jesus Christ, even him whom, notwithstanding all my present and now long-continued carelessness and wickedness, I still hold to be Jesus Christ my Lord. Oh! could my soul enter into the full meaning of these words as I would wish! But I hope that I shall be allowed this attainment by-and-by. Already my poor soul, in a manner hovering between time and eternity, cries, " NONE LIKE CHRIST! NONE BUT CHRIST FOR ME!" And may I, and all my relations and friends, be his henceforth and for ever! It is no small comfort to have my relations on earth so kind and agreeable to me; but my superlative desire, I think, is to be with Jesus and his ransomed millions above. That such a sinner, and originally such a mean sinner, should be kindly treated by so many brethren and friends, doth and may amaze me! But O how sweetly doth Jesus and his Spirit exceed them all! Now I, in some sweet measure, feel and see that there is no friendship like that of Father, Son, and Holy Ghost. This week my bodily appetite is no better; but little matter, if God would enable me to feed on Jesus' flesh—on all the fulness of God. At the meeting of the Synod let my weakness be represented to them; and if they judge that it has disqualified me for teaching the students, I heartily agree to be laid aside from this work, and that one more fit should be chosen. It is JESUS CHRIST whom I wish to be exalted; and the best means for saving sinners I wish to take place. I hope the brethren will take care to supply my congregation with sermon, as want of this would sink my spirits. I have been but a dry tree myself among them; and O it would rejoice my heart to hear of Jesus' power being felt, and his glory seen, by the ministry of my brethren helping me! I do not wish to be a burden to them; and if Providence bring me back unto any measure of strength, I shall inform the supplier. The longer I live, I see myself the less worthy of being regarded by anybody. Wishing all the blessings of time and eternity on your family, and that the Lord may render you and your brother, and all my pupils, more faithful, diligent, and successful in the ministry, than I have been, I remain yours, &c.

LETTER X.

DEAR ——,—I am, and have been since you went away, much as when you saw me. Still weak, but desiring to wait for the salvation of God; which I hope will make me strong in his due time. His afflicting hand lies very mercifully on me; how pleasantly his glorifying hand, in a short time, will lie on me, I with humility wish to know, as soon as it is for his glory, and my own and others good. O study early fellowship with Christ! It is sweet, in days of trouble, to look back to this. I hope that you will not grudge to preach for me another Sabbath; and may that sweet Jesus Christ, and his Spirit, give you and me many days of sweet fellowship with them; which I am sure and glad that they can give us. My allowed inclination is, to serve the Lord on earth or to praise him in heaven, as he thinks most for his honour for a time; though, saving his will, I would cheerfully prefer the latter. Oh! to be with Christ in heaven, appears to me a double, a triple heaven, for such a sinner! This, with my kind compliments to all my brethren about you.—Yours affectionately, &c.

LETTER XI.

EXTRACT OF A LETTER TO THE COUNTESS OF HUNTINGDON, SUPPOSED TO BE THE LAST HE WROTE TO HER.

IF I never write to you more, be these my last words: There is none like Christ, none like Christ, none like Christ; nothing like "redemption through his blood, even the forgiveness of sins, according to the riches of his grace." There is no learning nor knowledge like the knowledge of Christ; no life like Christ living in the heart by faith; no work like the service, the spiritual service of Christ; no reward like the free-grace wages of Christ; no riches nor wealth like "the unsearchable riches of Christ;" no rest, no comfort, like the rest, the consolations of Christ; no pleasure like the pleasure of fellowship with Christ. Little as I know of Christ, (and it is my dreadful sin and shame that I know so little of him,) I would not exchange the learning of one hour's fellowship with Christ for all the liberal learning in ten thousand universities, during ten thousand ages, even though angels were to be my teachers. Nor would I exchange the pleasure my soul hath found in a word or two about Christ, as, *thy* God, *my* God, for all the cried-up pleasures of creation since the world began. For what, then, would I exchange the being for ever with Christ, to behold his glory, see God in him as he is, and enter into the joy of my Lord?

MEDITATIONS.

MEDITATION I.

THE GRACE OF GOD AS MANIFESTED IN REDEMPTION.

LORD, what am I in myself? Dust and ashes; formed from nothing: I am "nothing, less than nothing, and vanity." But what am I as a sinner? An infinitely criminal enemy of God, my Maker, my Preserver, and Redeemer; whose heart is full of malice and hatred, and my life filled up with rebellion against him. My heart is the very reverse of all the excellency that is in God; my life a presumptuous trampling on all the authority, and an ungrateful contempt and abuse of all the kindness of God. In my heart there is the quintessence of all evil; it is harder than a flinty rock; more loathsome than a noisome carcass; more rotten than a long dead corpse; more noxious than a pestilential pit, or an unripe grave; more mischievous than a tiger or scorpion ; more ugly than a monster ; more proud, deceitful, and desperately wicked, than a devil. "O wretched man that I am ! who shall deliver me from the body of this death ? " Where sin abounded, indignation and wrath, tribulation and anguish, might have justly for ever abounded. Had I been in hell these many years, I had received only the due reward of my deeds ; but "where sin abounded, grace did much more abound." I have done all that I could to dishonour God ; and God doth all he can to save and exalt me. Grace how undeserved! how unasked! how refused and trampled on by me! But how dear to God! how strong! how unbounded in God! By the grace, the free favour of God, I am what I am. By his forbearing grace I am out of hell ; by his saving grace I am on my way to heaven; by grace I was chosen in Christ ; by grace I am redeemed to God by the blood of Christ; by grace I am pardoned, reconciled, and accepted in Christ ; by grace I am one in spirit with Christ ; by grace I am a child and heir of God in Christ; by grace I am quickened and fortified in Christ; by grace I am preserved and comforted in Christ; and by grace I shall quickly be glorified with and in Christ. What is this ! "Saved in the Lord with an everlasting salvation ! " Grace, grace unto it ! "Grace reigns through righteousness unto eternal life by Jesus Christ." Who is this Jesus Christ ? Immanuel, God with us ; the Son of God, in two distinct natures and one person for ever. What is Christ ? He is all in all, and all in all to me. I am a lost sinner ; Christ is my Saviour :—I am a captive, enslaved and miserable; Christ is my Redeemer:—I am an enemy to, and a rebel against God; Christ is the mediator between God and me:—I am a bankrupt infinitely indebted to God's law and justice; Christ is my surety that paid all my debt:—I am infinitely guilty before God; Christ is my atoning priest, and sacrifice, and ransom:—I am ignorant; Christ is my instructing prophet:—I am stubborn and rebellious; Christ is my all-subduing king:—I am a lost sheep; Christ is my shepherd:—I am destitute; Christ is my friend:—I am forsaken; Christ is my refuge and my helper:—I am blind; Christ is my light:—I am naked; Christ is my white raiment:—I am disobedient; Christ is my righteousness:—I am polluted; Christ is my sanctification, a fountain opened for sin and uncleanness:—I am grieved; Christ is my comforter:—I am poor; Christ is my wealth:—I am diseased; Christ is my physician:—I am dead; Christ is my life:—I am dying; Christ is my portion for ever. If I look through my Bible, Christ fills every page. He is the end of every genealogy, the centre of every history, the fulfilment of every law, the substance of every promise, the exemplification of every doctrine, and the accomplishment of every prophecy. If I look through creation, I see Christ the maker, Christ the preserver, Christ the end, Christ the centre and glory of all things. I see thousands of them bright emblems of my Christ! Oh, my soul! art thou also full of Christ?

MEDITATION II.

REDEMPTION! thou eternal excellency, thou joy of many generations, return, return, that I may look upon thee! How my heart is amazed, is ravished with the view of what my adored Jesus hath done for me in the *purchase* of redemption, and doth to me in the everlasting *application* of it to my soul! There, in the *purchase*, Jehovah found him out, and laid my help upon him who is mighty: here, in the *application*, he is found of me that sought him not. There he struck out my name from my debt-bond, the broken covenant—sad charter to infinite woe!—and inserted his own: here he " makes with me an everlasting covenant, even the sure mercies of David." There he made himself heir to my deserved threatenings of his Father's indignation: here he bequeaths, he gives to me his exceeding great and precious promises of eternal life. There, to be firmly connected with my guilt, my woe, he was made a priest with an oath: here, that I might have strong consolation, he swears that he hath " no pleasure in the death of the wicked," and that " surely blessing he will bless me."

There, in the *purchase* of redemption, he who "was in the form of God, and thought it not robbery to be equal with God," emptied himself of his glory: here, in the *application* of it, he confers upon me an " exceeding and eternal weight of glory." " The Lord is my everlasting light, and my God, my glory." There he was " found in fashion as a man," a son of man: here he makes me a son, " an heir of God, and joint-heir with Christ." There he was sent forth " in the likeness of sinful flesh:" here he makes me a " partaker of the divine nature," and changes me into the divine " image, from glory to glory." There he became " a worm and no man :" here he renders me " equal to the angels of God in heaven." There he, the Son of his Father's love, was an outcast, an exile : here, I, a hateful distant foe, am, through his blood, brought near unto God, even to his seat. There he bare our infirmities, was weary and weak-hearted : here he hath a fellow-feeling of our infirmities, is afflicted in all our afflictions, and perfects his strength in my weakness. There he " made himself of no reputation, was a reproach of men, and despised of the people :" here he gives me " a new name, which the mouth of the Lord doth name;"—the ransomed of the Lord; the holy one; " sought out, and not forsaken." There he took upon him the yoke of the broken law ; the yoke of my transgressions was wreathed about his neck : here he brings me into " the glorious liberty of the children of God;" puts on me " his yoke which is easy, and his burden which is light." There he " bore the sins of many; he was made sin for us :" here he makes me righteous, " the righteousness of God in him." There he was condemned, was made a curse for us : here he is " exalted a Prince and a Saviour, to give repentance and forgiveness of sins;"

"sent to bless me in turning me from mine iniqui-ties;" set up to be blessings for evermore. There he was joined with thieves, "was numbered with transgressors:" here he "puts me among the chil-dren;" joins me with "thrones and dominions, prin-cipalities and powers." And "truly my fellowship is with the Father, and with his Son Jesus Christ."

There, in the *purchase* of redemption, he was oppressed with ignominious poverty, had not where to lay his head: here, in the *application* of it, "through his poverty I am made rich;" he gives me his "unsearchable riches," "the goodly heritage of the hosts of nations;" fills me with "all the fulness of God;" gives me "the Most High for my habita-tion," my "dwelling-place in all generations." There "for hunger and thirst his soul fainted in him:" here he satiates my soul with goodness; gives me his "flesh, which is meat indeed, and his blood, which is drink indeed;" gives me the bread of life, living water, an overflowing cup of salvation. There he "hid not his face from shame and spitting;" had "his visage more marred than any man, and his form more than the sons of men:" here he makes me lift up my face without spot unto God; makes me "shine forth as the sun in the kingdom of my Father." There he was deserted of God; his Father forsook him, and was "far from the words of his roaring:" here he lifts on me the light of Jehovah's counte-nance, and shall make me like him, by seeing him as he is; for "so shall I be for ever with the Lord." There "he gave his back to the smiters, and his cheeks to them that plucked off the hair;' "was wounded for our transgressions, and bruised for our iniquities : " here he is the Lord my God " that healeth me;" " who healeth all my diseases," and " bindeth up my painful wounds;" and " by his stripes I am healed." There, from the cross, he would not come down and save himself : here, from the throne, he comes down to save me from " the pit of corruption," "draw me out of many waters, turn me from ungodliness, and save me from the lowest hell." There he wore "a crown of thorns :" here he gives me " a crown of life;" makes me " a royal diadem in the hand of my God." There he drank for me the baleful cup of infinite wrath : here he gives me " the fountain of life," " rivers of pleasure," " wine and milk, without money and without price," and makes me " draw water out of the wells of salvation." There he was amazed and very heavy, " exceeding sorrowful, even unto death : " here he makes me obtain " joy and gladness," go to God, " my exceeding joy," and " enter into the joy of my Lord." There he " poured out his soul unto death," travailed in pain till he knew not what to say : here he is formed in my heart " the hope of glory ; " sees in me " the travail of his soul, and is satisfied." There he shed his blood for me : here he " loves me, and washes me from my sins in his own blood, and makes me a king and priest unto God, even his Father." There he died for the ungodly : here he " hath quickened me, who was dead in trespasses and sins; " " because he lives, I shall live also; " " my life is hid with Christ in God; and when he appears, I shall appear with him in glory." There he was buried, descended into the lower parts of the earth : here, raised up and alive for evermore, he "raiseth me up together, and makes me sit together with him in heavenly places." What melting views are these! How my heart *heaves* with joy,—flames with love,—would burst in praise!—if wonder would allow.

MEDITATION III.

REFLECTIONS OF A SOUL SHUT UP TO THE FAITH.

LOOK back, my soul, " to the rock whence thou wast hewn." Ponder the manner in which Jehovah loved thee, and "delivered thee from the pit of corruption." How the fiery law, with its dread mandates all pointed against my sins ; and its tremendous penalty turned every way, to stop my escape from the graciously inviting God of infinite mercy. To what numerous, to what wretched shifts I betook myself, to shun the Redeemer! By a Christian education, God had shut me up from the more flagrant iniquities,—cursing, swearing, lewdness, intemperance, and the neglect of the forms of religion. But, ah ! with what earnestness I indulged myself in sins not less criminal, though less open and scandalous! When his law convinced my conscience that my " secret faults were set in the light of his countenance," and that what is " highly esteemed among

men is abomination in the sight of God," how eagerly
I turned aside to seek righteousness, " as it were by
the works of the law!" When conscience upbraided
me for neglect of former duties, particularly of acts
of worship, how often have I redoubled, or even
tripled the ordinary tale, in order to pay off my old
debts! How foolishly my heart cried, " Have patience with me, and I will pay thee all!" Still my
conscience, like " the daughter of the horse-leech,
cried, Give, give." The Lord thundered into my
soul, " As many as are of the works of the law are
under the curse; for it is written, Cursed is every
one that continueth not in all things written in the
book of the law to do them. Cursed is the man that
trusteth in man, and maketh flesh his arm, whose
heart departeth from the Lord." While I for many
days compassed Sinai, " going about to establish my
own righteousness," together with, or more truly in
opposition to, the righteousness of Christ, " the thunder waxed louder and louder." How then was " my
moisture turned into the drought of summer," and I
was " wearied in the greatness of my way!" How
plainly I perceived all my attempts towards virtue to
be the mire and dirt cast up from a troubled sea of
inward rage and enmity against God,—against the
Redeemer! How I trembled to feel myself reserved,
in chains of guilt, condemnation, and sinful pollution,
to the judgment of the great day! How oft my
agonized soul sobbed forth, " My bones are dried;
my hope is lost; and I am cut off for my part." Not
all the flames of Sinai could melt my heart. I hard-

M

ened myself in sorrow, and became more obstinate in inward rebellion against the Lord. "I went on frowardly in the way of my heart. I loved idols, and after them I would go."

But thanks be to God, that stopped my career! While I rolled and raged in my blood, without any eye to pity me, he passed by me, and looked upon me, and "said unto me, when I was in my blood,"—my devilish rage against the Redeemer,—"LIVE!" And, behold, "my time was the time of love"—the day of power—the day of espousals indeed! Determined to make an uncommon stretch of Almighty grace, he hedged me in. Before, behind, and on every side, I heard, I saw, I felt,—not cherubim with flaming swords, but calls, but cords, of everlasting love. Before me I saw, I heard "God in Christ reconciling the world unto himself," saying to my heart, "I am the Lord thy God." To silence every doubt, he sware unto me, "Hear, O my people! and I will speak; I will testify against thee. I am God, even thy God,"—as really, as fully thine, as I am God! Behold, I heard his voice, "Thou shalt have no other gods before me." I saw myself thus charged with all the authority of heaven, to take God, Father, Son, and Holy Ghost, in Christ, to be my God, and my all; and that neither blasphemy, nor murder, nor any thing horrid, could be more aggravated rebellion against him than my not believing that he was *my God ;* and that all conception, all worship of him, under any other view than as *my God,* was but the placing of an idol in his room! How my heart was

astonished to find that the first and great commandment so charged me, the chief of sinners, a very prince
of devils, to possess what the Lord God giveth me,—to
possess the INFINITE ALL, as in Christ, *my own*. When,
in humility produced from hell, I pled that I was not
worthy of him,—that I could not believe,—could
not receive him,—could not obey his sweet command,
—he took me by the arms, by the heart on every
side, and said, " I will be to them a God, and they
shall be to me a people. I will say, It is my people ;
and they shall say, The Lord is my God."

Thus encompassed on every side, tell me, ye sons
of men, ye powers of darkness, " what was I, that I
could withstand God ? " Had all the enmity in hell
been concentrated in my heart, how could it have
withstood such omnipotence of love ? how could I
have escaped out of God's hands ? how could I have
trodden on the " exceeding great and precious promise" and oath of God, confirmed with his blood ?
how could I have trampled on the great, the kind
commandment of infinite love ? how could I have
broke the arms of Almighty grace, which grasped me
hard ? how could my heart, my soul, forbear to cry
out, *Amen, so be it, Lord,*—to say of the Lord, " He
is my refuge and my fortress ; my God, in whom I
will trust,—*My Lord and my God ?* Lord, I believe,
help thou mine unbelief."

But will God indeed be *mine,* wholly mine !—for
ever mine ! Is the word,—the oath,—gone out of his
mouth, and sealed with his blood ? Cursed then be
every disposition, every thought of my soul that

dissents. Let the mouth of these liars be stopped. Lord, persecute and destroy from under these heavens this evil heart of unbelief;—thy curse upon it. But what shall I render to the Lord for his infinite gift of *himself* to *me?* Such as I am, Lord, I give myself to thee, as my God;—myself as *naked*, as *guilty*, I give to thee, as my God, my righteousness,—my God, that "covereth me with the robe of righteousness and the garments of salvation,"—my God, that "justifieth the ungodly" "freely by his grace, through the redemption that is in Christ Jesus,"—my God, unmatched in "forgiving iniquity, transgression, and sin;"—myself as *foolish* and *ignorant* I give to thee, as my God, my Redeemer, that "teacheth to profit,"—my God who hath "compassion on the ignorant," and "openeth the eyes of the blind," and maketh "the heart of the rash to understand knowledge,"—to my Christ, as "made of God to me wisdom;"—myself as *polluted* I give to thee, my God, that "saveth from all uncleanness,"—to thee, my Redeemer, who art come to Zion to "turn away ungodliness from Jacob,"—who art "a fountain opened for sin and for uncleanness,"—who art "made of God to me sanctification;"—myself as *rebellious* I give to thee, my "God of peace," who slays my enmity by the blood of his Son,—and to thee, O Jesus! who hath "received gifts for men, yea, for the rebellious also, that the Lord God may dwell among them," and "daily load them with his benefits;"—myself as *weak*, insufficient to think any thing, do any thing, spiritually good, I give to thee, my God, who "giveth power to the faint, and to them that have no might, increaseth strength,"—to thee, the worker in and for me of thy good pleasure;—myself as *poor* and *wretched*, as *poverty* and *emptiness* itself, I give to thee, my God, my *all*, and in all,—my God, who accounts it "more blessed to give than to receive," that thou mayest "supply all my wants out of thy riches in glory by Christ Jesus!"

MEDITATION IV.

REFLECTIONS OF A CHRISTIAN UPON HIS SPIRITUAL ELEVATIONS AND DEJECTIONS.

MY life is indeed "hid with Christ in God." My new-covenant state is "as Mount Zion, which can never be moved." But, ah! the instability of my spiritual condition! How often hath God lifted me up, and cast me down again!

Sometimes he hath lifted me up, in allowing me sweet distinct views of divine truth, and of Jesus and his Father therein. In his light I saw light, and walked, read, heard, and meditated, in "the light of his countenance!" Oh! my pleasing insight into the mystery of divine persons, and of divine perfections, as manifested in Christ;—into the mystery of redemption, in its rise, means, matter, and end;—and into my duty with relation thereto, even in intricate circumstances! Anon, he casts me down into deep and darksome caves. Ah! then, my ignorant, carnal, and mis-shapen apprehensions of divine things!

Amidst the best means of instruction, all were like a sealed book to my soul. I groped as a blind man at noon-day, neither understanding what was exhibited, nor whence I had come, nor whither I should go.

Sometimes God, by his Word and Spirit, afforded me the most convincing assurance that he was my Saviour, my Husband, my Father, my Friend, my Physician, my God,—my *all*, and *in all;* and enabled me to claim him in every character, in every promise, without the least hesitation. Anon, he permitted me to fall into such darkness and doubts, that I could be persuaded of scarce anything inspired. I doubted of, I disputed against, all his saving relations to me, all his promises of kindness to me. Even when he testified against me that he was God, even my God, I pleaded he was a liar. Oh, shocking! I resisted, rebelled against, and vexed his Holy Spirit!

Sometimes God hath lifted me up to a sweet serenity of soul. Like one beloved of the Lord, I dwelt in safety. No angry challenge from heaven, or from my own conscience, disturbed my repose. Even amidst troubles, or in the view thereof, I rested on the Lord, and quietly waited for his salvation. Anon, he cast me "into deep waters, where there was no standing." " All his waves and billows went over me." Ah! how "tossed with tempest, and not comforted!" While heaven deserted and frowned, while "the arrows of the Almighty stuck fast in me, and the poison thereof drank up my spirit,"—Satan trod me under his feet, sheathed in me thousands of his fiery darts; my raging corruptions wrought, and were tempestuous; the world hated, reproached, and persecuted me! Scarce aught remained, but "a fearful looking for of fiery indignation."

Sometimes God hath lifted me up, in so plentifully "shedding abroad his love in my heart," and so powerfully arresting my thoughts on divine things, that not all the temptations of Satan, or solicitations of the world, could draw it aside. My heart so burned with love to him, that it could desire nothing, care for nothing, and converse with nothing, but himself. Anon, it became so loose, so unfixed, that I could not for my soul confine it a moment to a spiritual object in a spiritual manner; but whole armies of idle, ignorant, legal, unbelieving, blasphemous, proud, covetous, malicious, or wanton thoughts, crowded into my mind!

Sometimes God, in lifting me up, hath inflamed my heart with the most ardent desires after himself. How my soul longed, hungered, thirsted, and panted for the Lord! How it cried and "followed hard after him!" Nothing could divert, nothing could check, my ardour in pursuit of him; and when I found him, I held him as with a death-grasp, and would not let him go. With what brokenness, what eagerness of heart, I wept, and made supplication to him! Anon, by casting me down, I could neither breathe after nor pray for his visits. I neither knew nor cared whether I found him or not. Nay, rationally sensible that "my Beloved had withdrawn himself and was gone," a stupid unconcern overpowered my heart: I was almost content to have his room filled with sinful pleasures and earthly enjoyments.

Sometimes God hath so lifted me up, enabling me to live on Christ himself, above dependence on sensible frames, that I rested on, and gloried in, his person, office, love, righteousness, intercession, power, and faithfulness, as the infallible security of my forgiveness, acceptance, sanctification, comfort, and eternal felicity, notwithstanding much felt guilt, temptation, and trouble. Anon, I have been so cast down, that my spiritual courage and hope altered as my inward frames did.

Sometimes I have been so lifted up, that I could with pleasure distinctly review my former noted enjoyments of Christ; how, when, and where, he appeared to my soul, loosed my bands, forgave my sins, quickened and feasted my soul. Anon, I have been so cast down, that I lost the impression of former experiences; could scarce discern whether they were from heaven or of men,—from heaven or from hell; and, alas! became strangely careless what was their nature, source, or tendency. Ah! how the promises, —the words of grace,—in which I had formerly " tasted that the Lord is gracious," became as idle tales, as a well without water, and as flinty rocks!

Sometimes " the zeal of his house,"—inflamed by the applications of redeeming love, and directed by his Word and Spirit,—" hath eaten me up." I counted nothing, no, not life itself, dear unto me, if I might have Jesus exalted, his truths believed and maintained, and his people increased in the earth. Anon, I have fallen under the power of so much selfishness, that, if I could get my own interest secured, I scarcely regarded the glory or the public honour of Christ.

Sometimes God hath filled " my mouth with his praise and honour all the day." I could not refrain from praise; I could not forbear commending him " whom my soul loveth;" I could not but, in a manner suited to my station, invite others to come, " taste, and see, that the Lord is good,"—could not but call such as feared God to hear " what he had done for my soul." Anon, a dumb devil hath taken possession of my heart; sinful bashfulness, confusion and carelessness, have quite disqualified me for conference on any spiritual subject,—nay, I felt a strong inclination to deal in trifles and calumny.

Sometimes God has so feasted me in his ordinances, that the frequent return of Sabbaths, sacramental occasions, opportunities of family, social, or secret worship, were my delight. Often I had him preengaged to vouchsafe his presence in this and that ordinance of his grace. Often the Angel of the covenant restrained the winds of temptation and floods of corruption, while he sealed my soul " to the day of redemption." Oh! how " he brought me into the banqueting-house, and his banner over me was love; how he stayed me with flagons, and comforted me with apples, while I was sick of love!" Anon, ordinances became to me as " dry breasts and a miscarrying womb." Ah! their approach seemed a trifle, a burden, to my careless, carnal heart; neither before, nor in, nor after, did I enjoy the visits of Christ. In my attendance, levity, legality, and unconcern, carried all before them. How oft the voice, the gesture, the method, of the administrator, took that room in my heart which pertained to Christ! Often disappointed of the presence of God, ah! how I sunk into mere formality, or doubts of my duty to attend! And at last, how often have I neglected worship altogether, if the hurry of the world seemed to call me to some other business.

Sometimes God hath carried me up to Mount Pisgah, and shown me the celestial Canaan, and my irrevocable title thereto, till my whole soul was transported with wonder, desire, and delight! How " I desired to depart and to be with Christ, which is far better!" How I groaned, " earnestly desiring to be clothed upon with my house which is from heaven!" Anon, he held back the face of his throne, and spread his cloud over it. Heaven was forgotten,—my interest therein was unseen. Nay, how oft hell presented itself as the heritage appointed to me by God!

Are thy frames, my soul, so changeable? Let me charge thee to have no confidence in thyself; but to live by faith on the Son of God, and his everlasting covenant, which are " the same yesterday, to-day, and for ever." Count " all things but loss, for the excellency of the knowledge of Christ Jesus, thy Lord; and but dung, that thou mayest win him, and be found in him, not having thine own righteousness which is of the law, but the righteousness which is of God by faith."

MEDITATION V.

REFLECTIONS OF A CANDIDATE FOR THE MINISTERIAL OFFICE.

Dost thou, my soul, desire " the office of a bishop of souls,"—a minister of Christ? Examine with deep concern thy preparation for, thy call to, and thy end in offering thyself to this important work.

Am I a real Christian? or am I a devil, a dissembler with God and men,—an entertainer of sin and Satan in my heart? Am I a new creature, having my corrupt nature renewed, old things having passed away, and all things become new? Do I " worship God in the spirit,"—read, meditate, pray, converse, under the influence of the Holy Ghost? Do I know and rejoice in what Christ is in himself, and what he is to and hath done for and in me? Have I " no confidence in the flesh"—in my own righteousness, my learning, my address? Hath the Holy Ghost emptied me of self, in every form, till he hath made me " poor in spirit," " less than the least of all saints" in my own sight? Hath he with a strong hand instructed me to " count all things but loss for the excellency of the knowledge of Christ Jesus my Lord ; and to count them but dung that I may win him, and be found in him, not having my own righteousness, but the righteousness which is of God by faith?" Do I earnestly desire to " know him, and the power of his resurrection, and the fellowship of his sufferings,"— and to " press toward the mark for the prize of the high calling of God in Christ Jesus" ? What furniture of gifts hath Christ bestowed upon me,—what aptness to teach,—what knowledge of " the mysteries of the kingdom,"—what skill to instruct others, " bringing forth out of my treasure things new and old,"—what ability to make the deep things of God plain to weaker capacities,—what quickness of conception,—what due inclination to study, as one devoted to matters of infinite consequence,—what peculiar fitness for the pulpit, qualifying me to " commend myself to every man's conscience in the sight of God," preaching not in the " enticing words of man's wisdom, but in demonstration of the Spirit, and with power"? With what stock of self-experience, texts, and principles of inspiration, am I entering on the solemn office? Of what truths, relative to the law of God and its threatenings, relative to sin, to Satan, and to divine desertion, hath my saddened soul felt the power, tasting " the wormwood and the gall"? Of what declarations and promises of grace have I tasted, and seen that God is good? What cords of infinite love have caught and held my heart? What oracles of heaven have I " found and eaten"? and have they been to me " the joy and the rejoicing of my heart"? Of what truths and what texts could I now say, " I believe, and therefore I speak"? " What I have heard with the Father,—what I have seen, and heard, and tasted, and handled, of the Word of life,—that I declare unto you."

Suppose my connections with the great, or my address to the people, should ever so easily procure me a licence, or a charge, yet, if I run unsent by Christ, I

must in my whole ministrations act the part of a thief,
a robber, a traitor to Christ, and a murderer of souls,
not profiting them at all. If without his commission
I enter the office, what direction, what support, what
comfort, what acceptance, what reward, can I expect
in and of my work ? Say then, my conscience, as thou
shalt answer at the judgment-seat of Christ, am I
" taking this honour to myself, or am I called of God,
as was Aaron" ? Is Christ sending me, and laying a
necessity upon me to preach the gospel ? While he
determines me to follow Providence, and to take no
irregular step towards thrusting myself into the office,
is he breathing on my soul, and causing me to " receive the Holy Ghost" ? Is he endowing me with
tender compassion for the souls of men ; and with a
deep sense of my own unfitness, and earnest desire to
be " sanctified, and made meet for the Master's use" ?
In the progress of my education, am I going " bound
in the spirit," with the love of Christ burning in my
heart, and constraining me ; rendering me willing
cheerfully to suffer poverty, contempt, and hatred of
all men, for his name's sake ; willing, if possible, to
risk my own salvation in winning others to Christ ?
What scriptures have directed and encouraged me to
this work ? In what form doth Jesus seem to be
giving me my commission ?—whether " to open the
eyes of the unconverted, and to turn them from darkness to light, and from the power of Satan unto God,
that they may receive forgiveness of sins, and an inheritance among them that are sanctified ;"—or to
" go, make the heart of this people fat, and their ears

heavy, and shut their eyes; lest they see with their eyes, and hear with their ears, and understand with their heart, and convert and be healed?" What promise of Christ's presence with, and assistance in, my work, have I received from above?

What is mine end in my advances towards this work? Dare I appeal to him that "searcheth my heart and trieth my reins,"—to him who will quickly be my Judge,—that I " seek not great things for myself;" that I " covet no man's silver, or gold, or apparel ; " that I " seek not theirs, but them ; " that " neither of men seek I glory ; " that I " look not on mine own things," but on the things of Christ; that I seek not mine own honour, but the honour of him that sends me?

Have I considered diligently what is before me, or am I running blindfold on the tremendous charge? Have I considered the nature and circumstances of the ministerial work;—that therein I am to be an " ambassador for Christ," to beseech perishing souls, on the brink of hell, to be " reconciled unto God," —a steward of the mysteries and manifold grace of God ;—that, at the infinite hazard of my soul, it is required of me to be faithful;—that, in my ministrations, I with " all humility and many tears " serve the Lord with my spirit in the gospel of his Son, keep back no part of the counsel of God,—no instruction, no reproof, no encouragement;—that I "testify repentance toward God, and faith toward our Lord Jesus Christ;" not moved with reproach, persecution, hunger, or nakedness ; nor even " count my life dear unto me, if so I may finish my course with joy;" "ready not to be bound only, but to die for the name of the Lord Jesus;" willing rather to be ruined with Christ, than to reign with emperors;—that I labour with much fear and trembling, determined to know, to glory in, and to make known, nothing but "Jesus Christ and him crucified;" "not with enticing words of man's wisdom, as a man-pleaser, but with great plainness of speech, in demonstration of the Spirit and with power;" speaking "the things freely given to me of God by his Spirit, not in the words which man's wisdom teacheth, but which the Holy Ghost teacheth, comparing spiritual things with spiritual, and having the mind of Christ;" "always triumphing in Christ, and making manifest the savour of his knowledge in every place; being to God a sweet savour of Christ in them that are saved, and in them that perish; as of sincerity, as of God, in the sight of God, speaking in Christ;" through the mercy of God, "not fainting, but renouncing the hidden things of dishonesty; not walking in craftiness, nor handling the word of God deceitfully, but by the manifestation of the truth to every man's conscience in the sight of God;" "not preaching myself, but Christ Jesus the Lord, and myself a servant to the Church for Jesus' sake; always bearing about the dying of the Lord, that his life may be made manifest in me"? "Knowing the terror of the Lord," and the judgment to come, I must "persuade men, making myself manifest to God and in their consciences." Constrained by the love of Christ, I must labour in every way to bring sinners to the Saviour; "travailing in birth till Christ be formed in them;" "jealous over them with a godly jealousy, and espousing them as chaste virgins to Christ." I must "take heed to my ministry which I have received of the Lord, that I fulfil it;" giving myself "to reading, to exhortation, to doctrine; taking heed to myself and to the doctrine, that I may save both myself and them that hear me;" "watching for their souls, as one that must give an account;" "rightly dividing the word of truth, and giving every man his portion in due season;" faithfully "warning every man, and teaching every man in all wisdom, that I may present every man perfect in Christ Jesus;" and warring, not after the flesh, nor with weapons that are carnal, "but mighty through God to the pulling down of strongholds, and casting down imaginations, and bringing into captivity every thought to the obedience of Christ." Having Christ Jesus "for the end of my conversation," and "holding fast the form of sound words in faith and love which is in him," I must "take heed unto myself, and to all the flock over which the Holy Ghost hath made me an overseer, to feed the Church of God which he hath purchased with his own blood;"—"taking the oversight thereof, not by constraint, but willingly; not for filthy lucre, but of a ready mind; neither as being a lord over God's heritage, but being an ensample to the flock," "exercised unto godliness," holy, just, and unblamable; "an example to the believers, in word, in conversation, in charity, in faith,

in purity;" "fleeing youthful lusts, and following
righteousness, faith, charity, peace; avoiding foolish
and unlearned questions; not striving, but being
gentle to all men,—in meekness instructing those
that oppose themselves;"—"avoiding perverse dis-
putings" and worldly-mindedness, as most dangerous
snares; "fighting the good fight of faith, and laying
hold on eternal life;"—"preaching the word, being
instant in season and out of season; reproving, re-
buking, exhorting, with all long-suffering and doctrine;"—keeping the trust of gospel truth and office
committed to me, and "committing the same to faithful men, who shall be able to teach others also."
And, in fine, to try false teachers; to rebuke before
all such as sin openly; to restore such as have been
overtaken in a fault, in the spirit of meekness; and,
having compassion on them, to "pull them out of the
fire, hating even the garment spotted by the flesh."

MEDITATION VI.

REFLECTIONS OF ONE ENTERED ON THE PASTORAL OFFICE.

PONDER, my soul, with solemn awe!—Am I without that God, that Christ,—a stranger to that covenant of promise, which I preach to others? While I
commend Jesus Christ from the pulpit, am I a de-
spiser of him in my heart? While I, in the name of
God, call on others to receive him as the "unspeakable gift" of God, am I rejecting him myself? Am I
daily occupied in preparing the gospel entertainment

N

for others, while I refuse to taste it myself? If my ends are selfish, or if I am not hearty in my work, how can God be expected to bless my labours? If in heart I am Satan's servant, how can I be true to Christ, or earnest for his honour? If I have not drunk deep of "the terrors of the Lord," the bitterness of sin, the vanity of the world, the importance of eternity, and of the conscience-quieting and heart-captivating virtue of Christ, how can I be serious and hearty in preaching the gospel? If I am not influenced by a predominant love to Christ; if I live not to him; if my heart is not fixed upon eternal things; if it pant not after fellowship with Father, Son, and Holy Ghost; and follow not eagerly holiness and peace, and prefer not the welfare of the Church to my chiefest joy in this world,—how can I, without the most abominable treachery and dissimulation, declare to others their chief happiness, and the proper methods to obtain it?

If I am a graceless preacher, how terrible is my condition! If I open my Bible, the sentence of my double damnation flashes on my conscience from every page. If I compose my sermon, I but draw up an awful indictment against myself. If I argue against men's sins, I but aggravate my own. If I speak of hell with its insupportable and everlasting torments, I but enfeoff myself therein, as the just portion of my cup, and my inheritance appointed me by the Almighty. If I speak of Jesus Christ and his excellencies, it is but to tread them under my feet. If I take his new covenant, and the fulness, the blessings

therein contained, into my mouth, it is but to profane them,—" to cast them out to be trodden under
foot of men." If while I hold up the glass of God's
law, and of his gospel to others, I turn its back to
myself, the gospel "is hid to me, that am lost; in
whom the god of this world hath blinded the mind
of me who believe not, lest the light of the glorious
gospel of Christ should shine" into my heart.

If I know not the Alpha and Omega, the truth,—
what is all my knowledge but an accursed puffer up
—a murderer of my soul! Ah! how my table, my
reading, my meditations, my sermons, my principles,
my prayers, as a trap and snare, take and " bind me
hand and foot, to cast me, the unprofitable servant,
into outer darkness;" with all my Bible, all my books,
all my gifts, as it were inlaid in my conscience, like
fuel, like oil, to enrage for ever the flames of infinite
wrath against my soul! Ah! am I set here, at the
gate of heaven, as a candle to waste myself in showing others the way,—in lighting up the Bridegroom's
friends; and must my lamp at the end go out in obscure darkness! If I die unfaithful to Christ, in what
a tremendous manner shall I for ever sink into the
bottomless pit, under the weight of the blood of the
Son of God, the Saviour of men,—under the weight
of murdered truths, murdered convictions, murdered
gifts, a murdered ministry, and murdered souls! How
shall I for ever curse myself, that I did not rather
choose to be a tinker, a chimney-sweeper, an execu-
tioner, than a pretended, a treacherous minister of
Christ! Vile, vile, accursed hypocrite, how shalt

thou "dwell with the devouring fire"! how shalt thou "dwell with everlasting burnings"!

Suppose I should even know "the grace of God in truth;" yet, if my graces are not kept lively,—if "my loins are not girt, and my lamp burning,"—all inflamed with Jesus' love constraining my heart,—how careless, how carnal, how blasted, how accursed, must my ministrations be! Ponder, my soul, the nature of thy work, as a dealing between the infinite God and the immortal, the perishing souls of men! Ponder the extent of thy duties, and the solemnity of thy engagements! Think how the honours and privileges of my office, and my relation to Christ therein, ought to instigate me to faithfulness! What self-denial, what pure regard to the honour of God, what prudence, what diligence, what humility, what zeal, what spirituality of heart and life, what entire dependence on Jesus by faith, what order, what plainness, what just tempering of mildness and severity, are necessary in thus dealing with the souls of men!

But ah! while I stand in the courts of the Lord, and minister in holy things in his name, how polluted and abominable are my heart and life! Ah! what lusts prevail! How dreadful the case of my hearers' souls, if it is like to mine! What if I have less of the life and reality of religion than the weakest, the most untender saint under my charge! Ah! how my "evil heart of unbelief departs from the living God"! Where, where is my faith in God? Where is my burning of heart, while Jesus speaks to me and "opens to me the

Scriptures"? Where are my love-pantings, my languishing, my cries for the Lord? Where is my habitual fellowship with Father, Son, and Holy Ghost,—my sitting under the Redeemer's "shadow with great delight, while his fruit is sweet to my taste"? Where is my constant "travailing in birth until Christ be formed" in the souls of men? Where are the agonies which my heart hath undergone, both in the night and in the day, while the saving, the sanctifying presence of God was denied to me or to my flock?

Nay, how often hath pride been almost all in all to me! How often hath it chosen my companions, my dress, my victuals! hath chosen my text, my subject, my language! How often hath it indited my thoughts, and to the reproach, the blasting of the gospel, hath decked my sermon with tawdry ornaments and fancies, as if it had been a stage-play! How often hath it blunted the sharp arrows of truth with its swollen bombast, or silken smoothness! In the pulpit how often hath pride formed my looks, my tone, my action, and kindled me into earnestness! How often hath it rendered me glad to hear subsequently my own applause, or provoked me with the news of my being contemned! Ah! how much of my labour is owing to pride, spurred on by the fame of learning, diligence, or sanctity! No wonder my labours, so much influenced by Satanical motives, do Satan's kingdom so little hurt! Think, too, my soul, if my pride never made me envy or wound the characters of such as differed from me, or outshined me,—if it never made me reluctant to receive reproof, especially from those of inferior station ! Think if pride is less inconsistent with real Christianity than drunkenness or whoredom !

How much a factious spirit prevails with me ! Did I never take up a religious principle in the way of factious contention ? Did I never undervalue the peace and unity of the Church ? Have I been afflicted with Zion in all her afflictions, as if they had been my own ? By proving my opponents in a controversy mistaken and erroneous, have I never, in respect of manner or end, pleaded the cause of the devil ? Did I never incline to have any destitute of the ordinances or influences of heaven, rather than my party should be dishonoured ?

Ah ! how slothful have I been in the work of the Lord,—in studying the matter of divine truths, and their connection with Christ and with one another,— or in delivering them to my hearers ! How slothful in sympathizing with, and helping such, as had no fixed gospel ministrations; or in devising and carrying on measures for the honour of Jesus, and the welfare of souls ! How often carnal interest hath marred my zeal for the interest of Christ ! Hence what temporizing with the laws and customs of the world ! What shrinking from duties that required much labour or expense ! What uncheerfulness in giving liberal alms, and backwardness to improve whatever I have, for the honour of Christ, and the welfare of men !

Awake, my conscience ! " What meanest thou, O sleeper !" Bestir thyself for thy God. Ah ! I tremble to think how my parents, who piously devoted and educated me to this work of the Lord; how the masters, the teachers, who prepared me for it,—how the seminaries of learning in which I was instructed, the years I have spent in study, the gifts which God hath bestowed on me, my voluntary undertaking of the work,—how all the thoughts, the words, the works of the Father, Son, and Holy Ghost, to promote our redemption,—how all the divine commandments, promises, and threatenings, which inculcate my duty,— all the examples of apostles, prophets, and faithful ministers; how all the leaves of my Bible, all the books in my closet, all the sermons I preach, all the instructions and exhortations I tender, all the discipline I exercise, all the maintenance I receive, all the honours which I enjoy or expect, all the testimonies I have given against the negligence of parents, masters, ministers, or magistrates, all the vows and resolutions I have made to reform, and all the prayers I have presented to God for assistance or success,— shall rise up against me in the day of the Lord, if I do this work deceitfully. Alas! " who shall live when the Lord doth this ? "

Think, my soul, did not the Holy Ghost, who is ready to furnish me with everything necessary,—did not God, put me into the ministry? Was it that I might waste devoted time, that I might tear his Church, mangle his truths, betray his honour, and murder the souls of men ? Is not my charge the *flock of God*; the flock of God, *purchased with his own blood?* Shall I destroy the Redeemer's property, attempt to frustrate the end of his death? Hath he died for souls? Shall I then think any thing too hard to be done for their salvation? Shall I not be willing to part with all, and put up with all, to win men to Christ? Was he crucified for them,—for me? And shall not I crucify my selfishness, my pride, my sloth, my concupiscence, to save myself, and them that hear me? How hard my work! While my own salvation is at stake, how deeply connected with my diligence and faithfulness is the salvation of multitudes! How the powers of hell set themselves against me and my office, in order that they may triumph over Christ and his Church in my fall! How many eyes of God, angels, and men, are upon me! Why then, conscience, do I speak of heaven or hell—of Jesus and his love—his blood—of the new covenant and its blessings—in so careless and sleepy a manner, when before and on every side of my pulpit, there are so many scores or hundreds of immortal souls suspended over hell by the frail thread of life, already in the hands of the devil, and hasting toward everlasting ruin—slain by the gospel of Christ! Why do not tears of deep concern mingle themselves with every sentence I utter, when multitudes, just plunging into damnation, and perhaps hearing the offer of mercy for the last time, are, in respect of need, crying with an exceeding bitter cry, "Help, minister, I perish, I perish; oh, pluck me as a brand out of the burning; help me to escape from the wrath to come!" How should I spend a moment of my devoted time in idle chit-chat, in useless reading, in unnecessary sleep! What if, meanwhile, some one of my charge drop into hell-fire, and commence his everlasting curses of me, for not doing more for his salvation! What shall I do if God riseth up to require their blood at my hand? How accursed that knowledge which I do not improve for the honour of Christ, the bestower! How accursed that ease which issues in the damnation of men! How accursed that conformity to the world which permits my hearers to sleep hell-ward in sin!

MEDITATION VII.

REFLECTIONS OF A MINISTER ENCOURAGING HIMSELF IN CHRIST.

HAVE I obtained mercy? Hath the Son of God loved me, and given himself for me? Hath he translated me " out of darkness into his marvellous light"? Hath he called me, and furnished me with knowledge, with spiritual experiences, for my work? Let me show forth the praises of him who hath called me. "Why art thou cast down, O my soul? Hope thou in God, for I shall yet praise him, who is the health of my countenance, and my God." Hath he separated me to the gospel of the grace of God— " counted me faithful, putting me into the ministry," and giving me, "who am less than the least of all saints, this grace, that I should preach among the Gentiles, the unsearchable riches of Christ"?

Let me "magnify mine office." He hath raised me from the dunghill, and exalted me above "prin-

cipalities and powers, thrones and dominions," to
be a stated preacher of Christ,—an ambassador and
herald of the Lord of hosts. How delightful my
employment, to survey, to tell out, " the exceeding
riches of Christ,"—all my own!—to publish " exceeding great and precious promises," all given to
me!—to declare to my brethren " his name, which
is as ointment poured forth"!—to proclaim "redemption through his blood, the forgiveness of sins, according to the riches of his grace"!—to be ever,
" with joy, drawing water out of the wells of salvation"! to be a worker together with God in the
chief of all his ways, the salvation of men!—to be
like angels, "always beholding the face of my Father
who is in heaven"!—to be " all the days of my life
dwelling in the house of the Lord;" " beholding his
beauty, and inquiring reverently in his temple"! to
be measuring the " length and breadth, and depth
and height, and to know the love of Christ, which
passeth knowledge, and to be filled with all the
fulness of God"!

Let me, therefore, be "in nothing terrified by my
adversaries," nor by the arduous nature of my work.
In the full assurance that Jesus is mine, and hath
called me, let no distress, no persecution, no danger,
move me. Jesus, "the forerunner, is for me entered
within the veil." He, " the breaker, is gone up before me;" he hath broken up and passed through;
" he is at my right hand, I shall not be moved;" he
sendeth none "a warfare upon his own charges;" he
hath said to my soul, "Lo! I am with thee alway,

even unto the end of the world. As thy days are, so shall thy strength be. My presence shall go with thee, and I will give thee rest. When thou passest through the waters I will be with thee; and through the rivers, they shall not overflow thee. When thou walkest through the fire, thou shalt not be burnt; neither shall the flame kindle upon thee. Fear not, I am with thee; be not dismayed, I am thy God. I will give you another Comforter, that he may abide with you for ever, even the Spirit of truth. He shall teach you all things, and bring all things to your remembrance. He shall take of mine, and shall show it unto you. When he is come, he will convince the world of sin, and of righteousness, and of judgment. Be thou faithful unto death, and I will give thee a crown of life. To him that overcometh will I grant to sit with me on my throne, even as I also overcame, and am set down with my Father on his throne."

Bestir thyself, my soul; let me walk in the light of the Lord; let me "set my face like a flint." Let me go forth in his strength, to promote the salvation of souls, that they may be my hope, my joy, my glory, my crown of rejoicing in the day of the Lord. Nay, though sinners "be not gathered, yet shall I be glorious in the eyes of the Lord; my judgment shall be with the Lord, and my work with my God." Is Jesus my surety, my sacrifice, my teacher, my Lord, my friend, my father, my husband, my Saviour, my God, my glory? Let me "indite good matter touching the King." Let " my tongue be as the pen of a ready writer." Let Jesus be the end of all my ministrations. If "I seek to please men, I cannot be the servant of Christ." If I chiefly regard my own honour, my humour, or my temporal advantage, how shall I hold up my face to Him "who loved me, and gave himself for me"! If he is the beloved Son of God, "full of grace and truth," for men, for me,—and "made of God to us wisdom, and righteousness, and sanctification, and redemption,"— let it be my great aim to promote the glory of his grace, in the salvation of all around me ; and to be "a sweet savour of Christ unto God in them that are saved, and in them that perish." If I display the perfections of God, let it be as they shine "in the face of Jesus Christ." Let Jesus, in his person, natures, offices, relations, works, and blessings, be the matter of my ministrations. Let me exhibit laws, doctrines, promises, and threatenings, in due connection with him ; the law as a covenant fulfilled and magnified by him, and driving men to him ; the law as a rule, consecrated by his blood, founded on his atonement, and requiring the improvement of him as our all and in all; the promises as yea and amen in him, the new covenant in his blood. If I exhibit the blessings of salvation, let me represent them as purchased with his blood, lodged in his heart, and distributed by his bountiful hand ; and as blessings wherewith the Father blesseth men in Christ Jesus. If I point forth the providences of God, let it be as the doing of my Lord, and marvellous in my eyes. If I proclaim the terrors of the Almighty, let them appear as the punishment appointed for such as "tread under foot the Son of God, and count the blood of the covenant an unholy thing;" as the condemnation of the obstinate rejecters of God's unspeakable gift. If I call men to repent, let it be in "looking to Jesus," whom they have pierced. If I inculcate prayer, let it be as a coming "boldly to the throne of grace," in the view of having " a great high priest, Jesus the Son of God." If I recommend thanksgiving, let it be chiefly for Christ, and acceptable through him. If I press the duties of the law of any kind, let it be as part of Christ's purchased salvation, as the fruits of faith living on Christ; as enforced by the authority and the love of Christ; and produced under the influence of Christ, and his Spirit dwelling in us; as conducive to the glory of Christ; and acceptable only through his merits and intercession. Let every particular duty be enforced with some particular consideration of Christ, 1 Cor. vi. 8–11, 15 ; 2 Cor. viii. 9 ; Tit. ii. 11–14 ; Rom. xiii. 14; Eph. iv. 22, 25, 32. Let my very style savour of Christ, manifesting great plainness and energy, and drawn from the oracles of Christ.

Since Jesus hath put me into this dignified office, and hath assured me of his assistance and reward, let me show myself " a workman that needeth not to be ashamed, rightly dividing the word of truth," and giving every one his meat in due season, in correspondence to their respective stations, conditions, and inclinations. Let me so preach the grace of the gospel, as to promote an humble and universal dependence on Christ; but meanwhile condemn the sluggish and careless professor. Let me labour to screw into every man's conscience the divine truths suited to his case. Let me distinctly explain and enforce particular duties, and oppose particular lusts and vices. After searching my own heart, and much prudent pains to understand the spiritual condition of the various persons of my charge, let me labour so to apply my doctrines, that every one may know himself and his circumstances before God; so as the ignorant may be instructed, scoffers and gainsayers convinced, the stupid and secure awakened, the slothful roused and excited, the legalist and moralist have his hopes slain, the hypocrite may feel his "covering too narrow to wrap himself in," the afflicted may be comforted, the wanderer reclaimed, and the sincere asker of the way to Zion may be directed.

In fine, "holding fast the form of sound words, in faith and love which is in Christ Jesus,"—and "keeping that good thing"—office, gifts, and grace—"committed to me by the Holy Ghost which dwelleth in me,"—let me carefully lay the foundation, in a frequent and pointed explication of gospel truth relative to Jesus' person and righteousness, and the sinner's union with him, and justification through his imputed atonement. Let me, in the most clear and convincing manner, point out the nature and circumstances of regeneration and turning to God,—together with the marks of a gracious state, and the difference between a spiritual and saving change of the heart effected by the Holy Ghost, and the counterfeits thereof. In nothing let me study more accuracy than in explaining the nature, progress, and circumstances of gospel sanctification.

————

DYING ADVICE TO HIS YOUNGER CHILDREN.

My Dear Children,—Believing that God hath made with me, and with my seed after me, his " everlasting covenant, to be a God to me and to my seed," I did, in your baptism, and often since, and now do, before God and his angels, make a solemn surrender of you all into the hands of my God, and my father's God, and of the God of your mother, and her father's God; and in the presence of that God, and as ye shall answer at his second coming, I charge you,—

1. To learn diligently the principles of our Christian and Protestant religion, from your Catechisms and Confession of Faith, but especially from your Bible. God's word hath a light and life, a power and sweetness in it, which no other book hath, and by it your souls must be quickened and live, or you must be damned for ever; and the more closely you press the words of the Bible to your own hearts, and pray and think them over before God, you will find them the more powerful and pleasant. My soul hath found inexpressibly more sweetness and satisfaction in a single line of the Bible—nay, in two such words as these, *Thy God* and *my God*—than all the pleasures

found in the things of the world, since the creation, could equal.

2. Give yourselves to prayer. Jesus hath said, "Suffer little children to come unto me, and forbid them not: for of such is the kingdom of heaven." "I love them that love me; and those that seek me early shall find me." "Remember now thy Creator in the days of thy youth." "The Lord is good to the soul that seeketh him." He is the hearer of prayer, and therefore to him should "all flesh come." The Lord, "the Father of the fatherless," takes an especial pleasure in hearing the prayers of the fatherless young ones.

When I was left destitute of a father, and soon after of a mother, the Lord dealt so with me; and though I was too bent on childish diversions, the Lord, on some occasions, made prayer more pleasant to me than any of them. By prayer improve the Lord as your Father, consulting him and asking his direction in all your ways, and seeking his blessing on your learning, and on whatever you do agreeable to his will.

3. Study earnestly to love, honour, and obey your mother, and to be a comfort to her. Much trouble hath she had in bringing you so far in the world, and much affection hath she showed you. She hath now a double charge and authority over you. The Lord now observes particularly what is done to her. Oh! for the Lord's sake, do not dishonour her, or break her heart, by your disobedience and graceless walk;

otherwise the Lord's dreadful curse will light upon you, and ye will readily soon perish : for think what God hath said, Prov. xvii. 25, " A foolish son is a grief to his father, and bitterness to her that bare him." Chap. xx. 20, " Whoso curseth his father or his mother, his lamp shall be put out in obscure darkness." See also Deut. xxi. 18, 19 ; Prov. x. 1, xiii. 1, xv. 5, 20, xix. 13, 26, xxviii. 7, 24, xxx. 17.

4. Avoid as plagues, every light, frothy, and wicked companion. Be not a disgrace to me, and cause of damnation to yourselves, by keeping company with idle talkers, swearers, drunkards, tipplers, frothy or lewd persons. Scarce any thing more infallibly brings persons to misery in this world, or to hell in the next, than loose and trifling companions. Prov. xiii. 20, " He that walketh with wise men shall be wise ; but a companion of fools shall be destroyed." Chap. xxviii. 7, " Whoso keepeth the law is a wise son; but he that is a companion of riotous men shameth his father." See also Prov. i., ii., v., vi., vii., and ix., and 1 Cor. v. 9, 11. Never make any your companions with whom you would not wish to appear at the judgment-seat of Christ, and with whom you would not wish to live for ever.

5. Mind earnestly the infinitely important concerns of your eternal salvation. I hereby constitute the Addresses annexed to my Shorter and Larger Catechisms a part of my dying directions to you. Oh ! ponder and practise them ! Wo to you if, by your carelessness and wickedness, you thrust the grace of

God out from among my posterity! Ah! my dear
young children, shall I at the last day have to echo
my *Amen* to Christ's sentence of your eternal damnation? In order to stir up your concern about
eternal things, let me beseech you to read Boston's
Fourfold State, Pearse's Best Match, Rutherford's
Letters, Guise's Sermons to Young People, Alleine's
Alarm, and Baxter's Call; but beware of some legal
directions in the last two. Read also the lives of
Elizabeth Cairns, of Alexander Archibald, and especially the lives of Messrs Thomas Halyburton, James
Frazer, and James Hogg. Perhaps, also, my Journal
may be useful to you; but above all, read the *Book
of Inspiration.*

6. Never affect conformity to the vain and vile
fashions of this world : if you do, you disobey God,
and hazard the ruin of your own souls. Rom. xii. 2,
"Be not conformed to this world, but be ye transformed by the renewing of your mind." James iv. 4,
"Know ye not that the friendship of the world is
enmity with God? whosoever therefore will be a
friend of the world is the enemy of God." See also
1 Cor. vii. 31; 1 John ii. 15–17, iv. 5, 6, v. 4, 19;
John vii. 7, xv. 18, 19; Psal. xv. 4, cxxxix. 21,
cxix. 53, 115, 136, 158.

7. Never marry, nor take one step towards marriage, without much serious and solemn consultation
of God, and patient waiting for his direction. By
means of rash marriages was the old world defiled;
and it was partly on this account that it was drowned,
Gen. vi. In consequence of following these examples,

Esau's posterity were cast out from the Church of God to all generations, Gen. xxvi. 34, 35; Judah's family was disgraced and killed, and it is to be feared that his two sons perished, Gen. xxxviii; not only Jehoshaphat's family, but even the kingdom of Judah was almost ruined, 2 Chron. xxi., xxii. How dreadful for your own souls, and for those of your children, if you take into your bosom an unconverted lump of wrath! For the Lord's sake, let no beauty, no affability, no wealth, decoy any of you into this dangerous snare, which may exclude the grace of God from your family till the end of time, 1 Cor. vii. 39; Deut. vii. 3, 4; Ezra ix. 2, 3, 12, 14.

8. If the Lord give you families and children, bring them up for God. I have essayed to point out your duty in this respect, in my two sermons at Whitburn and Inverkeithing, which were printed: I pray you seriously to peruse these, and to comply with the advices given in the same.

9. Set the Lord always before you as your Saviour, Witness, Master, Pattern, and future Judge. David saith, Ps. xvi. 8, "I have set the Lord always before me : because he is at my right hand, I shall not be moved." It is the command of God, 1 Cor. x. 31, " Whether therefore ye eat or drink, or whatsoever ye do, do all to the glory of God."

10. Adhere constantly, cordially, and honestly to the Covenanted principles of the Church of Scotland, and to that testimony which hath been lifted up for them. I fear a generation is rising up, which will endeavour silently to let slip these matters, as if they

were ashamed to hold them fast, or even to speak of them. May the Lord forbid that any of you should ever enter into this confederacy against Jesus Christ and his cause!

This from a dying father and minister, and a witness for Christ,

JOHN BROWN.

THE END.